NIHONGO NO KISO I

KAIGAI GIJUTSUSHA KENSHŪ KYŌKAI

This is the romanized edition of NIHONGO NO KISO I

Edited by
Kaigai Gijutsusha Kenshū Kyōkai
(The Association for Overseas Technical Scholarship)
30-1, Senju Azuma 1-chōme, Adachi-ku, Tōkyō, 120 Japan

Published by
3A Corporation
Shoei Bldg.
6-3, Sarugaku-cho 2-chome, Chiyoda-ku, Tokyo, 101 Japan
Printed in Japan

序

　財団法人海外技術者研修協会は，1959年に設立されて以来アジア・アフリカ・ラテンアメリカの発展途上諸国の技術研修生の受入れおよび研修の事業を行なってきた。研修生数は1980年3月末現在，延べ17,526人にのぼっている。

　研修生は当然のことながら日本の社会の中で生活し，日本の企業で実地の技術研修を受けるわけであり，彼らにとっての最大の悩みは言葉である。日本語が分からなければ日本の生活になじめないし，技術の習得も十分には望めない。私たちの経験では研修の成果と日本語習得の度合いとは，多くの場合，比例関係にあるということができる。このような日本語の重要性に鑑み，協会では研修生が工場実習にはいる前に，一般研修の一環として日本語教育を行なっている。

　協会の日本語教育は最初3週間コースとして発足したが，1961年から5週間コースに拡充されて現在に至っている。時間にして約100時間である。言葉の教育としては異例なほどの短時間であるが，これは研修生の滞在期間が極めて限られているためであり，私たちはこの中でもっとも効率的な，そして具体的な成果のあがる方法を工夫しなければならない。

　そこで1961年，協会独自の教科書「Practical Japanese Conversation」が作られた。その後1964年に改訂版，1965年に2訂版が出された。しかし受入研修生数は年々増加し，その教育程度も多様化し，また対象国もおよそ100か国，使用言語もまちまちとなってきたため，この教科書はかならずしも実情にそぐわないものとなった。

　そのため1967年には，あらたな構想のもとに「実用日本語会話」(Practical Japanese Conversation) を作成した。1969年にはそのスペイン語，タイ語，中国語，韓国語，およびインドネシア語版も完成した。ところが，この「実用日本語会話」は日本語の基礎文法をほぼ網羅し，語彙にして約1300語を含む内容の教

科書であったため，協会で行なう100時間の短期集中教育の教科書としては，やや複雑すぎるきらいがあった。

　こうして，私たちはさらに2年半の検討を加え，内容，体裁ともに新しい教科書を編纂することになった。それがこの「日本語の基礎」である。

　この教科書は，協会が対象とする技術研修生のための5週間コース用として編纂されたものであるが，教科書の説明を読みその指示に従うならば，一般の短期学習者，あるいは入門期の日本語教育にも十分活用できるであろう。各方面の助言を得て，今後さらに改善の努力を続けたい。

凡　　例

教科書の編集方針

1.　この教科書は，もともと財団法人海外技術者研修協会受入れの研修生のために作成されたものであるが，同時に広く一般の日本語学習を希望する人々のためにも十分役立つように作成されたものである。

　　この教科書は，始めて日本語を学ぶ人々に対して，日本語の基本文法と語彙の学習を通して，最終的には日常生活に必要な会話力を習得させることを目標としている。従って，ひらがな，かたかな及び漢字の指導，又は，日本文の読み書き指導等は原則として含まない。

2.　この教科書は，本来，日本人の教師の指導のもとで短期間に集中的に学習し，最大の効果をあげるよう編集されたもので，理論よりも実用性を重んじた。従って，使われた文型及び語彙は，まず基本的であること，使用頻度が高いことの他に，初学者にとって理解しやすいこと，発話しやすいことを重視して選択したものである。従って，日本人の間で使用頻度が高くても，かならずしもこの教科書にとりいれていないものもある。

3.　この教科書は，発話文型中心に構成されている。発話文型とは，日常かわされている日本語の会話の様々な表現を，話し手の立場からいくつかの主要な文の型に整理したものである。これらの発話文型を十分な口頭練習を通じて定着させ，学習者の実践的会話力を養成するというのが，この教科書の基本的考え方である。

教科書の構成

1.　この教科書は，本冊，分冊，文法解説書及び別冊付録の４つに分かれる。

　　本冊は序，凡例，研修生のみなさんへ，日本語の発音，本課，日本の歌，索引及びチャートからなり，本課は30課で構成される。

　　分冊は本課の各課毎の新出語彙とその翻訳，本冊の翻訳及び付表からなる。

　　文法解説書は本冊中の日本語の発音及び本課30課の各課における文法事項についての英文による文法説明である。

　　別冊付録は本冊の各課における練習問題の模範解答である。

2.　本冊はローマ字版と漢字まじりひらがな版の２種類があり，いずれも翻訳は一切含まない。教師は，教室では主に本冊を用いて，できるだけ媒介語を使わないで授業をすすめることが望ましい。

　　分冊は，英語，インドネシア語，タイ語，スペイン語，ペルシャ語，アラビヤ語及び韓国語版，中国語版，ベトナム語版，及びポルトガル語版に分かれる。

3.　各課の文型及び語彙は，学習者の理解力及び記憶力を考慮して選択，配列したもので，すべて必須である。

　　語彙は合計763語で，原則として各課の文例（文型，会話，例文，練習，問題）中にあらわれたものが中心であるが，その他，特に各文型に関係の深い語彙も付け加えられ

ている。新出語彙は前半の課に比較的多く，後半，動詞の変化が複雑になるにつれて少なくしてある。

4.　この教科書を教室で用いると，一課を完全に終わるのに少なくとも3時間はかかる。従って，一日一課ずつ進むものとして，発音課と本課を全部修了するには，最低5週間の期間と，延べ100時間の授業時間が必要となろう。

教科書の使い方

1.　本冊

　1)　日本語の発音

　　　本課にはいる前に，1～2時間かけて練習する。

　2)　本課

　　A.　1～27課

　　　各課は6頁で構成され，内容は以下のように分けられる。

　　　ⓐ文型

　　　　その課で学ぶ基本文型を，新出語彙を含まない平叙文で表わしたものである。学習者はここにあげられた例文を構造的に十分理解し，できれば暗記することが望ましい。

　　　ⓑ会話

　　　　その課の文型に日常よく使われる慣用的表現を適宜加えて作成した。実用的で，場面に応じた平易な会話であるから，全文暗記することが前提である。

　　　ⓒ例文

　　　　基本文型を，質問及び答えという対話の形式で表現したものである。学習者は，まず質問に応じてすみやかに答えられるよう練習を重ね，次に平叙文を与えられて，その質問形が即座に言えるように訓練されなければならない。

　　　ⓓ練習

　　　　文型をほとんど反射的に発話できるようにするための口頭文型練習である。授業で用いる時は，学習者は本を閉じて，教師の指示に従って練習しなければならない。教室外でも，テープを通して口頭で練習することが望ましい。練習の主なタイプは次の3つである。

　　　　　①　代入ドリル

　　　　　②　変換ドリル

　　　　　③　質問ドリル

　　　　また，練習はAとBに分かれる。練習Aには基本的な代入ドリルと変換ドリルが，視覚的効果を考えて並べてある。練習Bは代入や変換ドリルのやや複雑なもの，答え方を指定した質問ドリル，及び，代入と質問の混合ドリルが主なものである。

　　　ⓔ問題

その課の文法事項を確認するための問題と，文型に沿った問答形式の質問である。文法問題については問題をよく読んで正しい答えを書けばよいが，問答形式の質問は，最終的には耳で聞いて理解し，口頭で答えられなければならない。

　　ⓕ復習

　　　24課と26課に，それぞれ助詞と後続句の復習問題がある。

　B．28〜30課

　　　　28課 — 助詞のまとめ

　　　　29課 — 後続句のまとめ

　　　　30課 — 品詞の変換のまとめ

　　主な助詞は1〜13課までに提示されるので，13課終了後に28課を参照することが望ましい。

　　主な後続句は13〜19課で提示されるので，19課終了後に29課を参照することが望ましい。

　　30課の内容はほとんど新出事項で，それ以前の課と直接的関連が薄いが，20〜27課の間の適当な時間に言及することが望ましい。

　3）　チャート

　　　チャートは指定されたドリルを行なう時に用いる。

2．　分冊

　1）　各課別語彙とその各国語訳

　　　学習者は各課の語彙をすべて，その日のうちに暗記しなければならない。

　2）　本冊の各課別文型，会話及び例文の各国語訳

　　　翻訳は理解のための補助手段であって，学習者に翻訳を要求してはならない。ただし，日本語を発話させるための練習に翻訳を利用することはさしつかえない。

　3）　付表

　　　①　数字，時の表現，助数詞及び家族の名称

　　　②　動詞の変化表

　　　以上の内容は本冊でも扱われるが，範囲が広く，網羅されていないのでここで整理した。

3．　文法解説書

　　　各課の基本的な文法事項を項目毎に図式を多くとり入れて英文で簡潔な説明を行なったものである。

4．　別冊付録

　　　原則として学習期間中は教師が預かり，学習者はこれを見てはいけない。問答形式の質問の答え方は人によって違ってくるが，ここでは解答者をインドネシアのスラメットと定めて，答えを書いてある。

5．　表記上の注意　—ローマ字版—

　1）　ローマ字表記は，原則として修正ヘボン式に従っている。長母音は，"ii"を除い

て母音の上に "‒" をつけた。

    e. g. a—ā,   u—ū,   e—ē,   o—ō,   ただし,   i—ii

2) 文の書きはじめ，および固有名詞と言語名の語頭は大文字で書いた。

    e. g. Lee-san, Chūgoku, Nagoya, Indoneshia-go

3) 接頭語，接尾語，助数詞等はハイフンでつないだ。

    e. g. o-shigoto, Tanaka-san, 25-sai

4) 外来語及び国名は，日本語の発音に従って表記した。

    e. g. tape-recorder→tēpu-rekōdā, Mexico→Mekishiko

5) 人名は，その国で用いられている慣用的ローマ字表記に従った。

6. その他

1) 省略と言い換え

文中，省略できる語句は [ ] でくくった。

    e. g. Anata wa kenshūsei desu ka. —Hai, [watashi wa] kenshūsei desu.

文中，別の語句でも言い換えられる場合はその語句を （ ） でくくって，言い換え可能な部分の次に示した。

    e. g. Anata wa dare (donata) desu ka.

2) この教科書に出てくる国名及び人名は，ほとんどアジア，アフリカそしてラテンアメリカの発展途上国に限られている。理由は，この教科書がもともと協会が対象とする技術研修生のために作成され，使用されているからである。

3) 教科書の中に頻繁に出てくるセンター (Sentā) という名称は，海外技術者研修協会の各センター，すなわち東京研修センター，横浜研修センター，関西研修センター，および中部研修センターを指す。それぞれの所在地は目次の前に示されている。

学習者のみなさんへ

1. **文型をくりかえし練習しましょう。**

　日本語に限らず，新しい言葉を学ぶ際に文法の知識は大切ですが，それにあまりとらわれてはいけません。会話の一番の上達法は，まず日常よく使われている日本語の表現を，一定の文の形として理解し，覚えることです。この教科書では，文法事項や単語が，文型や会話の中にはいっていて，それらをくりかえし練習することでみなさんの会話力が自然に伸び，身につくように工夫してあります。

2. **正しい発音を聞いてください。**

　教科書の文字は，かならずしも実際の音を伝えていません。まず，先生やテープの声を聞いて，正しい発音を確かめてから覚えてください。単語であれ，文であれ，聞いて覚えるのが，もっとも早くて，確実な方法です。

3. **授業時間を最大に活用してください。**

　語学の勉強は教室の中だけに限られませんが，一番有効なのは何といっても，教室で先生について学ぶことです。この教科書は，100時間で日本語の基礎を能率よく，系統的に勉強できるよう構成されています。各課が新しい内容で，毎日毎日が大切ですから，授業中は先生の話しに耳を傾け，先生の指示に従って大きな声で練習してください。

4. **復習を怠らないでください。**

　教室の中だけで全部理解し，覚えることは，到底無理です。また，一度にたくさんの内容を丸暗記しても，すぐ忘れてしまいます。ですから，その日習った事は，クラスが終わってからも，テープなどを聞いて自分で発声しながら，できるだけ長い時間をかけて復習してください。一般的に言って，3時間クラスで勉強すれば，そのあと3時間の復習が必要です。

5. **覚えること，使うことが肝心です。**

　言葉の勉強の基本は，覚えること，そして，使うことです。まず，各課の単語と会話を覚えましょう。そして，覚えた言葉や文を使って，すぐ友だちや一般の日本人に話しかけてください。恥ずかしがっていては，決して上手になりません。

6. **この教科書が終わってから**

　1～5に述べた事を忠実に実行してこの本を終えると，日本語の基本的な表現と，日常生活に必要な基本的語彙を習得したことになります。そして，それらを上手に組み合わせて使えば，みなさんが話したいことの大半は表現できるはずです。

　ただ，最初のころは日本人の話す日本語が聞きとれなかったり，知らない言葉が多すぎたりして困るかもしれません。しかし，根気よく話し，聞き，そして言葉を覚えることを続けてください。そうすれば，かならず分かるようになります。

1. TKC (Tokyō Kenshū Center)

2. YKC (Yokohama Kenshū Center)

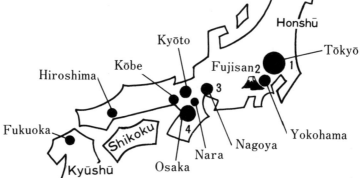

Sapporo   Hokkaidō

Honshū

Kyōto   Tōkyō
Kōbe   Fujisan 2
Hiroshima   1
                        3
Fukuoka   Shikoku   Yokohama
          4   Nagoya
Kyūshū   Osaka   Nara

3. CKC (Chūbu Kenshū Center)

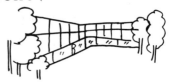

4. KKC (Kansai Kenshū Center)

Okinawa

MOKUJI

Nihon-go no Hatsuon

I. Nihon-go no onsetsu

a	i	u	e	o
ka	ki	ku	ke	ko
sa	shi	su	se	so
ta	chi	tsu	te	to
na	ni	nu	ne	no
ha	hi	fu	he	ho
ma	mi	mu	me	mo
ya	(i)	yu	(e)	yo
ra	ri	ru	re	ro
wa	(i)	(u)	(e)	(o)

kya	kyu	kyo
sha	shu	sho
cha	chu	cho
nya	nyu	nyo
hya	hyu	hyo
mya	myu	myo
rya	ryu	ryo

ga	gi	gu	ge	go
za	ji	zu	ze	zo
da	(ji)	(zu)	de	do
ba	bi	bu	be	bo
pa	pi	pu	pe	po

gya	gyu	gyo
ja	ju	jo
bya	byu	byo
pya	pyu	pyo

n

1. Boin

a	i	u	e	o
ā	ii	ū	ē	ō

tokei : tōkei, yuki : yūki, ojisan : ojiisan
obasan : obāsan, koko : kōkō, doro : dōro

2. "n" no hatsuon

onna, undō, antei
shinbun, sanpo, bunmei
sankai, kangaemasu

3. Nijū shi'in

oto : otto, shite imasu : shitte imasu
hakkiri, kippu, motto, issai

4. Shi'in + ya, yu, yo

hyaku, kyaku, ryokō, gyūnyū
kyūkō, byōki, sangyō, nyūsu

5. "za, zu, zo" to "ja, ju, jo"

zasshi, jama, zubon, jūsho, zōsen, jōdan
kazu, sanjū, kōzō, kōjō

6. "su" to "tsu"

isu : itsu, kasu : katsu, Suzuki : tsuzuki

II. Kyōshitsu no kotoba

1. Hajimemashō.
2. Owarimashō.
3. Yasumimashō.
4. Wakarimasu ka.
   —Hai, wakarimasu.
   —Iie, wakarimasen.
5. Issho ni dōzo.
6. Mō ichido [itte kudasai].
7. Chotto matte kudasai.
8. [Shitsumon ni] kotaete kudasai.
9. Kekkō desu.
10. Dame desu.

III. Sūji

1 — ichi
2 — ni
3 — san
4 — shi, yon
5 — go
6 — roku
7 — nana, shichi
8 — hachi
9 — ku, kyū
10 — jū

IV. Aisatsu

1. Ohayō gozaimasu.
2. Konnichiwa.
3. Konbanwa.
4. Oyasuminasai.
5. Sayōnara.

Dai 1 Ka

Bunkei

1. Watashi wa Lee desu.
2. Anata wa Tanom-san desu ka.
3. Tanom-san wa Nihon-jin dewa arimasen.
4. Rao-san mo kenshūsei desu.

Kaiwa

Tanom: Ohayō gozaimasu.
　　　　Watashi wa Tai no Tanom desu.
　　　　Tōkyō-kikai no kenshūsei desu.
　　　　Dōzo yoroshiku.
Tanaka: Dōzo yoroshiku.

Reibun

1. Anata wa kenshūsei desu ka.
   —Hai, [watashi wa] kenshūsei desu.
   —Iie, [watashi wa] kenshūsei dewa arimasen.

2. Anata wa Tanom-san desu ka.
   —Hai, [watashi wa] Tanom desu.
   Anata wa sensei desu ka.
   —Iie, [[watashi wa] sensei dewa arimasen,] kenshūsei desu.

3. Anata wa dare (donata) desu ka.
   —[Watashi wa] Lee desu.

4. Tanom-san wa Nihon-jin desu ka, Tai-jin desu ka.
   —[Tanom-san wa] Tai-jin desu.

5. Anata wa Indo-jin desu ka.
   —Hai, sō desu.
   Lee-san mo Indo-jin desu ka.
   —Iie, [sō dewa arimasen,] Lee-san wa Chūgoku-jin desu.

6. Anata-gata wa Burajiru-jin desu ka.
   —Iie, [watashi-tachi wa] Mekishiko-jin desu.

Renshū A

1. Watashi wa | Tanaka | desu.
   - Nihon-jin
   - sensei
   - Rao
   - Indo-jin
   - kenshūsei

2. Anata wa | Tanaka-san | desu ka.
   - Kimura-san
   - Lee-san
   - Tanom-san
   - dare (donata)

3. Watashi wa | Lee | dewa arimasen.
   - Arora
   - sensei
   - kenshūsei
   - Tai-jin
   - Iran-jin

4. Anata wa | sensei | desu ka, | kenshūsei | desu ka.
   - Indo-jin | Pakisutan-jin
   - Mekishiko-jin | Burajiru-jin
   - Rao-san | Ali-san

5. Watashi | mo kenshūsei desu.
   - Anata
   - Rao-san
   - Slamet-san

Renshū B

1. Rei: Watashi wa Nihon-jin desu.
    —Watashi wa Nihon-jin dewa arimasen.
    1) Anata wa sensei desu. —
    2) Watashi wa kenshūsei desu. —
    3) Anata wa Lee-san desu. —
    4) Lee-san wa Chūgoku-jin desu. —
    5) Tanom-san wa Tai-jin desu. —

2. Rei: Tanom-san wa kenshūsei desu ka.
    —Hai, Tanom-san wa kenshūsei desu.
    (Slamet-san, Ali-san, Rao-san, Arora-san, Abebe-san)

3. Rei: Anata wa Lee-san desu ka.
    —Iie, watashi wa Lee dewa arimasen, ... desu.
    (Kimura-san, Cortez-san, sensei, Nihon-jin, Chūgoku-jin)

4. Rei: Rao-san mo kenshūsei desu ka.
    —Hai, Rao-san mo kenshūsei desu.
    (Ali-san, Arora-san, Tanom-san, Slamet-san, Lee-san)

5. Rei: Tanom-san wa Indo-jin desu ka.
    —Iie, Tanom-san wa Indo-jin dewa arimasen, Tai-jin desu.
    (Nihon-jin, Marēshia-jin, Chūgoku-jin, Iran-jin, Echiopia-jin)

6. Rei: Rao-san wa Tai-jin desu ka, Indo-jin desu ka. (Indo-jin)
    —Rao-san wa Indo-jin desu.
    1) (kenshūsei, sensei   :   kenshūsei)
    2) (Indo-jin, Chūgoku-jin   :   Indo-jin)
    3) (sensei, kenshūsei   :   kenshūsei)

7. Rei 1: Anata wa kenshūsei desu ka. (hai)
   —Hai, watashi wa kenshūsei desu.

   Rei 2: Anata wa sensei desu ka. (iie)
   —Iie, watashi wa sensei dewa arimasen.

   1) Tanaka-san wa sensei desu ka. (hai) —
   2) Anata wa Nihon-jin desu ka. (iie) —
   3) Rao-san wa kenshūsei desu ka. (hai) —
   4) Anata mo kenshūsei desu ka. (hai) —
   5) Kimura-san mo kenshūsei desu ka. (iie) —
   6) Anata-gata wa Nihon-jin desu ka. (iie) —

8. Rei 1: Anata wa Slamet-san desu ka. (hai)
   —Hai, sō desu, Slamet desu.

   Rei 2: Anata wa Rao-san desu ka. (iie)
   —Iie, sō dewa arimasen, ... desu.

   1) Slamet-san wa Indoneshia-jin desu ka. (hai) —
   2) Slamet-san wa sensei desu ka. (iie) —
   3) Anata wa Lee-san desu ka. (iie) —
   4) Anata wa kenshūsei desu ka. (hai) —
   5) Tanom-san wa Tai-jin desu ka. (hai) —
   6) Rao-san mo Tai-jin desu ka. (iie) —

9. Chāto 1
   1) Rei: Tanom-san wa Tai-jin desu ka. — Hai, Tai-jin desu.
   2) Rei: Abebe-san wa Iran-jin desu ka. — Iie, Echiopia-jin desu.
   3) Cortez-san wa Burajiru-jin desu ka. —
   4) Kimura-san wa Nihon-jin desu ka. —
   5) Lee-san wa Chūgoku-jin desu ka. —
   6) Rao-san wa Pakisutan-jin desu ka. —
   7) Slamet-san wa Indoneshia-jin desu ka. —
   8) Garcia-san wa Ōsutoraria-jin desu ka. —
   9) Tanaka-san wa Kankoku-jin desu ka. —

Mondai

I. Rei: Anata wa (kenshūsei) desu ka.
          —Hai, kenshūsei desu.

    1. Anata wa (   ) desu ka.
        —Hai, watashi wa Lee desu.

    2. Rao-san wa (   ) desu ka.
        —Iie, sensei dewa arimasen.

    3. Slamet-san wa Indoneshia-jin desu.
        Anata mo (   ) desu ka.
        —Hai, sō desu.

    4. Cortez-san wa (   ) desu ka,
        Burajiru-jin desu ka.
        —Mekishiko-jin desu.

    5. Anata wa sensei desu ka, (   ) desu ka.
        —Watashi wa kenshūsei desu.

    6. Tanom-san wa (   ) desu ka.
        —Iie, Tanom-san wa Indo-jin dewa arimasen,
            Tai-jin desu.

    7. Anata wa (   ) desu ka.
        —Watashi wa Tanaka desu.

    8. Anata wa (   ) desu ka.
        —Iie, Ali dewa arimasen.

    9. Sensei wa (   ) desu ka, Chūgoku-jin desu ka.
        —Nihon-jin desu.

   10. Anata-gata wa (   ) desu ka.
        —Iie, watashi-tachi wa Nihon-jin dewa arimasen.

II. Rei: Anata wa kenshūsei desu ka.
          —Hai, watashi wa kenshūsei desu.

    1. Anata wa Nihon-jin desu ka.

    2. Anata wa sensei desu ka, kenshūsei desu ka.

    3. Abebe-san wa Echiopia-jin desu.
        Anata mo Echiopia-jin desu ka.

    4. Anata wa Lee-san desu ka.

    5. Anata wa donata desu ka.

Dai 2 Ka

Bunkei

1. Kore wa hon desu.
2. Sore wa watashi no hon desu.
3. Are wa sensei no desu.
4. Kono hon wa Tanom-san no desu.
5. Watashi wa 25[-sai] desu.

Kaiwa

Lee: Watashi no kagi o kudasai.
Kimura: Nan-ban desu ka.
Lee: 3-1-8 desu.
Kimura: Chotto matte kudasai.
          Hai, dōzo.
          Kore wa anata no shinbun desu ka.
Lee: Hai, sō desu. Watashi no desu.
          Dōmo arigatō gozaimasu.
Kimura: Dō itashimashite.

Reibun

1. Are wa nan desu ka.
   —[Are wa] haizara desu.

2. Sore wa dare no kaban desu ka.
   —[Kore wa] Tanom-san no kaban desu.

3. Kono jisho wa anata no desu ka.
   —Hai, [sono jisho wa] watashi no desu.
   —Iie, [sono jisho wa] watashi no dewa arimasen.

4. Kono pen wa dare no desu ka.
   —[Sono pen wa] Tanaka-san no desu.

5. Ano jisho wa Tanaka-san no desu ka, Rao-san no desu ka.
   —[Ano jisho wa] Rao-san no desu.
   Sore mo Rao-san no jisho desu ka.
   —Iie, [kore wa Rao-san no dewa arimasen,] Tanom-san no desu.

6. Anata wa o-ikutsu (nan-sai) desu ka.
   —[Watashi wa] 34 [-sai] desu.

7. Anata no senmon wa nan desu ka.
   —[Watashi no senmon wa] kikai desu.

Renshū A

1. Kore wa | hon | desu.
   haizara
   shinbun
   hako

   nan .... ka.

2. Are wa | tabako | dewa arimasen.
   kagi
   matchi
   kami

3. Sore wa | jisho | desu ka, | hon | desu ka.
   zasshi   shinbun
   bōrupen   enpitsu
   tsukue   isu

4. Kore wa | anata | no kaban desu.
   ano hito
   Kimura-san
   Garcia-san

   dare .... ka.

5. Sore wa | sensei | no desu.
   Tanom-san
   Ali-san
   watashi

   dare ...... ka.

6. Kono | pen | wa watashi no desu.
   jisho
   kaban
   nōto

Renshū B

1. Chāto 2

   1) Rei: Kore wa <u>kagi</u> desu ka.
      —Hai, [sore wa] <u>kagi</u> desu.

		4)	(haizara)	7)	(jisho)
2)	(pen)	5)	(nōto)	8)	(isu)
3)	(kami)	6)	(hako)	9)	(tsukue)

2. Chāto 2

   1) Rei: Sore wa <u>shinbun</u> desu ka. (shinbun)
      —Iie, [kore wa] <u>shinbun</u> dewa arimasen, <u>kagi</u> desu.

		4)	(tabako)	7)	(zasshi)
2)	(enpitsu)	5)	(jisho)	8)	(hako)
3)	(hon)	6)	(kaban)	9)	(mado)

3. Chāto 2

   1) Rei: Are wa nan desu ka. (kagi)
      —[Are wa] <u>kagi</u> desu.

		4)	(haizara)	7)	(jisho)
2)	(pen)	5)	(nōto)	8)	(isu)
3)	(kami)	6)	(hako)	9)	(tsukue)

4. Chāto 2

   1) Rei: Kore wa nan desu ka. (kagi) — Kagi desu.
   2) Rei: Kore wa bōrupen desu ka. (iie)
      —Iie, sō dewa arimasen, pen desu.
   3) Kore wa zasshi desu ka. (iie) —
   4) Kore wa tabako desu ka, haizara desu ka. (haizara) —
   5) Kore wa nōto desu ka. (hai) —
   6) Kore wa nan desu ka. (hako) —
   7) Kore wa zasshi desu ka, jisho desu ka. (jisho) —
   8) Kore wa tsukue desu ka. (iie) —
   9) Kore wa nan desu ka. (tsukue) —

— 13 —

5. Rei: Kore wa Rao-san no jisho desu ka.
　　　—Hai, [sore wa] Rao-san no jisho desu.
　　(Arora-san, Abebe-san, sensei, ano hito, ano kenshūsei)

6. Rei 1: Kore wa anata no desu ka. (hai) — Hai, watashi no desu.
　　Rei 2: Sore wa Ali-san no desu ka. (iie)
　　　　　—Iie, Ali-san no dewa arimasen, watashi no desu.
　　1) Are wa Lee-san no desu ka. (hai) —
　　2) Sore wa sensei no desu ka. (iie) —
　　3) Kore wa Tanom-san no desu ka. (iie) —
　　4) Are wa anata no desu ka. (iie) —
　　5) Kore wa Slamet-san no desu ka. (hai) —

7. Chāto 3

　　1) Rei: Kore wa dare no hon desu ka.
　　　　　—[Sore wa] watashi no hon desu.

	4) (matchi)
2) (enpitsu)	5) (rajio)
3) (kaban)	6) (terebi)

　　7) Rei: Kono zasshi wa dare no desu ka.
　　　　　—[Sono zasshi wa] Tanom-san no desu.

	10) (kamera)
8) (tokei)	11) (tabako)
9) (shinbun)	12) (jidōsha)

8. Chāto 1

　　Rei: Tanom-san wa o-ikutsu desu ka. (27)
　　　　　—Nijū-nana-sai desu.
　　1) (Abebe-san　　　:　　39)
　　2) (Lee-san　　　　:　　53)
　　3) (Rao-san　　　　:　　41)
　　4) (Slamet-san　　：　　21)
　　5) (Kimura-san　　：　　18)

Mondai

l. 1. Kore wa (   ) desu ka.
   —Hai, hon desu.

   2. Sore wa (   ) desu ka.
   —Jisho desu.

   3. Sore wa (   ) no kagi desu ka.
   —Lee-san no desu.

   4. Ano kaban mo (   ) no desu ka.
   —Iie, are wa Lee-san no dewa arimasen.

   5. Kono jisho wa (   ) no desu ka.
   —Hai, watashi no desu.

   6. Are wa enpitsu desu ka, (   ) desu ka.
   —Pen desu.

   7. Anata no senmon wa (   ) desu ka.
   —Watashi no senmon wa denki desu.

   8. Ano hito wa (   ) desu ka.
   —Arora-san desu.

   9. Arora-san wa (   ) desu ka.
   —Nijū-ichi desu.

   10. Sono hon wa (   ) desu ka.
   —Kimura-san no desu.

II. Rei: kore kaban no desu watashi wa
         —Kore wa watashi no kaban desu.

   1. nan wa ka are desu

   2. desu kagi ka dare sore no wa

   3. anata kono desu wa jisho no

III. 1. Anata no namae wa nan desu ka.

   2. Anata wa o-ikutsu desu ka.

   3. Anata no senmon wa nan desu ka.

   4. Anata wa Indoneshia no kenshūsei desu ka.

   5. Anata no sensei wa dare desu ka.

Dai 3 Ka

Bunkei

1. Jimusho wa asoko desu.
2. Shokudō wa sochira desu.
3. Koko wa kyōshitsu desu.
4. Kore wa terebi no hon desu.
5. Kore wa 1,500-en desu.

Kaiwa

Cortez:　Konnichiwa.

Rao:　　Konnichiwa.

Cortez:　Anata no kaisha wa doko desu ka.

Rao:　　Yokohama-denki desu.

Cortez:　Dewa, anata no senmon wa rajio desu ka.

Rao:　　Iie, chigaimasu. Terebi desu.

Cortez:　Sō desu ka.

　　　　Lee-san to onaji desu ne.

Reibun

1. Otearai wa doko desu ka.
    —[Otearai wa] soko desu.

2. Jimusho wa dochira desu ka.
    —[Jimusho wa] achira desu.

3. Rao-san wa doko desu ka.
    —[Rao-san wa] jimusho desu.

4. Matchi to haizara wa doko desu ka.
    —Matchi wa koko desu. Soshite haizara wa robii desu.

5. Koko wa doko desu ka.
    —[Koko wa] Kyōto desu.

6. Anata no o-kuni wa doko (dochira) desu ka.
    —[Watashi no kuni wa] Indo desu.

7. Anata no kaisha wa doko (dochira) desu ka.
    —[Watashi no kaisha wa] Nagoya-jidōsha desu.

8. Sore wa doko no tokei desu ka.
    —[Kore wa] Suisu no tokei desu.

9. Sore wa nan no hon desu ka.
    —[Kore wa] jidōsha no hon desu.

10. Kore wa ikura desu ka.
    —[Sore wa] 2,000-en desu.

Renshū A

1. Jimusho wa koko desu.
    soko
    asoko
    doko .... ka.

2. Shokudō wa kochira desu.
    sochira
    achira
    dochira .... ka.

3. Lee-san wa asoko desu.
    uketsuke
    niwa
    doko .... ka.

4. Koko wa kyōshitsu desu.
    Kenshū Sentā
    Kyōto

5. Kore wa kikai no hon desu.
    denki
    jidōsha
    nan .... ka.

6. Are wa Nihon no jidōsha desu.
    Amerika
    watashi no kuni
    doko .... ka.

7. Sore wa Nihon-go no jisho desu.
    Ei-go
    Supein-go

Renshū B

1. Rei: Otearai wa doko desu ka. (asoko)
   　　　—[Otearai wa] asoko desu.]
   　　1) (shokudō　　　　:　　　soko)
   　　2) (jimusho　　　　:　　　asoko)
   　　3) (Slamet-san　　　:　　　soko)
   　　4) (haizara　　　　:　　　koko)
   　　5) (shinbun　　　　:　　　asoko)

2. Rei: Terebi wa doko desu ka. (shokudō)
   　　　—[Terebi wa] shokudō desu.
   　　1) (isu　　　　　　:　　　kyōshitsu)
   　　2) (Rao-san　　　　:　　　niwa)
   　　3) (kenshūsei　　　:　　　robii)
   　　4) (denwa　　　　:　　　uketsuke)
   　　5) (anata no uchi　 :　　　Yokohama)

3. Rei: Uketsuke wa dochira desu ka. (achira)
   　　　—[Uketsuke wa] achira desu.
   　　1) (otearai　　　　:　　　kochira)
   　　2) (jimusho　　　　:　　　sochira)
   　　3) (kyōshitsu　　　:　　　achira)
   　　4) (shokudō　　　　:　　　achira)
   　　5) (Kenshū Sentā　 :　　　kochira)

4. Rei: Kore wa nan no hon desu ka. (denki)
   　　　—Denki no hon desu.
   　(kikai, jidōsha, terebi, rajio, Nihon-go, kagaku)

5. Rei: Kore wa doko no zasshi desu ka. (Nihon)
   　　　—Nihon no zasshi desu.
   　(Chūgoku, Firipin, Tai, Burajiru, Kankoku)

— 19 —

6. Rei: Sore wa nan no hon desu ka. (denki)
   —Denki no hon desu.
   1) (zasshi   :   kamera)
   2) (jisho   :   Nihon-go)
   3) (hon   :   kagaku)
   4) (kaisha   :   jidōsha)
   5) (nōto   :   Nihon-go)

7. Chāto 1

   Rei: Tanom-san no kuni wa doko desu ka. (Tai)
   —[Tanom-san no kuni wa] Tai desu.
   1) (Cortez-san   :   Mekishiko)
   2) (Kimura-san   :   Nihon)
   3) (Lee-san   :   Chūgoku)
   4) (Slamet-san   :   Indoneshia)
   5) (Garcia-san   :   Firipin)

8. Rei: Kore wa doko no zasshi desu ka. (Ōsutoraria)
   —Ōsutoraria no zasshi desu.
   1) (tokei   :   Suisu)
   2) (shinbun   :   Burajiru)
   3) (kamera   :   Nihon)
   4) (tabako   :   Igirisu)
   5) (jidōsha   :   Amerika)

9. Chāto 3

   Rei: Hon wa ikura desu ka. (1200) — Sen-nihyaku-en desu.
   1) (enpitsu   :   15)
   2) (zasshi   :   160)
   3) (tokei   :   23600)
   4) (rajio   :   16500)
   5) (kamera   :   37800)

Mondai

I. Rei: (Robii wa doko desu ka.)
      —Robii wa <u>asoko</u> desu.

  1. (   )
     —Tanom-san wa <u>uketsuke</u> desu.

  2. (   )
     —Otearai wa <u>achira</u> desu.

  3. (   )
     —Sore wa <u>gohyaku-en</u> desu.

  4. (   )
     —Kore wa <u>jidōsha</u> no hon desu.

  5. (   )
     —Watashi no kuni wa <u>Firipin</u> desu.

  6. (   )
     —Cortez-san no kaisha wa <u>Ōsaka-kagaku</u> desu.

  7. (   )
     —Kore wa <u>Nihon</u> no tokei desu.

  8. (   )
     —Watashi no kaban wa <u>heya</u> desu.

II. Rei: ((Kore), Koko, Kono) wa hon desu.

  1. Kyōshitsu wa (kono, koko, kore) desu.

  2. (Sore, Soko, Sono) kagi wa (watashi, watashi wa, watashi no) desu.

  3. Tanaka-san wa (Nihon-jin, Nihon-go, Nihon) desu.

  4. Rao-san (soshite, to) Arora-san wa Indo-jin desu.
     (Soshite, To) Tanom-san wa Tai-jin desu.

III. 1. Anata no o-kuni wa dochira desu ka.

  2. Anata no kaisha wa dochira desu ka.

  3. Anata no tokei wa ikura desu ka.

  4. Anata no heya no kagi wa doko desu ka.

  5. Anata no kaisha wa nan no kaisha desu ka.

Dai 4 Ka

Bunkei

1. Ima 1-ji 10-pun desu.
2. Watashi wa asa 6-ji han ni okimasu.
3. Watashi wa 9-ji kara 5-ji made hatarakimasu.
4. Watashi wa kinō benkyō-shimashita.

Kaiwa

Ali: Konbanwa.
Tanaka: Konbanwa.
           Dōzo kochira e.
           Ocha wa ikaga desu ka.
Ali: Hai, arigatō gozaimasu.
Tanaka: Ashita no benkyō wa nan-ji kara desu ka.
Ali: 8-ji han kara desu.
Tanaka: Nan-ji made desu ka.
Ali: 5-ji made desu.
Tanaka: Sore wa taihen desu ne.

Reibun

1. Ima nan-ji desu ka.
  —[Ima] 9-ji 5-fun desu.

2. Anata wa yoru nan-ji ni nemasu ka.
  —[Watashi wa yoru] 11-ji ni nemasu.

3. Anata wa ashita hatarakimasu ka.
  —Hai, [watashi wa ashita] hatarakimasu.
  —Iie, [watashi wa ashita] hatarakimasen.

4. Anata wa kinō benkyō-shimashita ka.
  —Hai, [watashi wa kinō] benkyō-shimashita.
  —Iie, [watashi wa kinō] benkyō-shimasendeshita.

5. Anata wa nan-ji kara nan-ji made yasumimasu ka.
  —[Watashi wa] 12-ji kara 1-ji han made yasumimasu.

6. Anata wa kinō no ban nan-ji made benkyō-shimashita ka.
  —[Watashi wa kinō no ban] 11-ji made benkyō-shimashita.

7. Getsu-yōbi no tsugi wa nan-yōbi desu ka.
  —[Getsu-yōbi no tsugi wa] ka-yōbi desu.

Renshū A

1. Ima 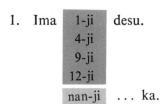 desu.

   nan-ji ... ka.

2. Watashi wa asa | 6-ji | ni okimasu.
   | 6-ji 10-pun |
   | 6-ji 15-fun |
   | 6-ji han |

   Anata wa .... nan-ji .... ka.

3. Watashi wa | 8-ji han | kara | 4-ji han | made hatarakimasu.
   | getsu-yōbi | | kin-yōbi |
   | asa | | ban |

4. Benkyō wa | 9-ji | kara | 12-ji | made desu.
   | 8-ji han | | 5-ji |
   | nan-ji | | nan-ji | .... ka.

5. Watashi wa | ashita | benkyō-shimasu.
   | asatte |
   | konban |
   | kinō | benkyō-shimashita.
   | ototoi |
   | kesa |

6.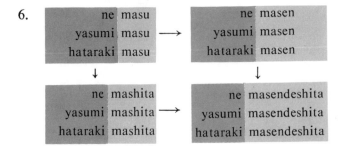

Renshū B

1. Chāto 4A

    1) Rei: Ima nan-ji desu ka. (9-ji)
         —Ima <u>ku-ji</u> desu.

		7)	(3-ji)
2)	(10-ji)	8)	(4-ji)
3)	(11-ji)	9)	(5-ji)
4)	(12-ji)	10)	(6-ji)
5)	(1-ji)	11)	(7-ji)
6)	(2-ji)	12)	(8-ji)

2. Chāto 4B

    1) Rei: Ima nan-ji desu ka. (4 : 05)
         —Ima <u>yo-ji go-fun</u> desu.

		6)	(4 : 40)
2)	(4 : 10)	7)	(4 : 55)
3)	(4 : 15)	8)	(chōdo 5 : 00)
4)	(4 : 30)	9)	(gozen 5 : 00)
5)	(4 : 35)	10)	(gogo 9 : 00)

3. Chāto 4A

    1) Rei: Anata wa nan-ji ni nemasu ka. (9-ji)
           —<u>Ku-ji</u> ni nemasu.
    2) (10-ji)
    3) (11-ji)
    4) (12-ji)
    5) (1-ji)
    6) (2-ji)

4. Chāto 4A

    I. Rei: Anata wa ashita nan-ji kara nan-ji made benkyō-shimasu ka.
         (9-ji, 3-ji) — <u>Ku-ji</u> kara <u>san-ji</u> made benkyo-shimasu.
   II. (10-ji, 4-ji)
 III. (11-ji, 5-ji)
 IV. (12-ji, 6-ji)
  V. (1-ji, 7-ji)
 VI. (2-ji, 8-ji)

5. Rei 1: Kyō hatarakimasu ka. (hai) — Hai, hatarakimasu.
   Rei 2: Gogo benkyō-shimasu ka. (iie) — Iie, benkyō-shimasen.
   1) Yoru hatarakimasu ka. (iie) —
   2) Yoru benkyō-shimasu ka. (hai) —
   3) Ashita benkyō-shimasu ka. (iie) —
   4) Nichi-yōbi ni hatarakimasu ka. (iie) —
   5) Kyō no gogo nemasu ka. (hai) —

6. Rei: 8-ji ni nemasu. (kinō no ban)
        —Kinō no ban 8-ji ni nemashita.
   1) 9-ji kara benkyō-shimasu. (kinō) —
   2) 6-ji ni okimasu. (kesa) —
   3) 3-ji made benkyō-shimasu. (kinō no ban) —
   4) 9-ji kara 5-ji made benkyō-shimasu. (ototoi) —
   5) 1-ji kara 3-ji made yasumimasu. (kinō no gogo) —

7. Rei 1: kyō hatarakimasu — kyō hatarakimasen
   Rei 2: kinō benkyō-shimashita — kinō benkyō-shimasendeshita
   1) ototoi hatarakimashita —
   2) ashita yasumimasu —
   3) konban nemasu —
   4) kinō no ban benkyō-shimashita —
   5) kesa 6-ji ni okimashita —

8. Rei 1: Kinō benkyō-shimashita ka. (hai)
           —Hai, benkyō-shimashita.
   Rei 2: Kinō hatarakimashita ka. (iie)
           —Iie, hatarakimasendeshita.
   1) Kinō hatarakimashita ka. (hai) —
   2) Kinō no asa benkyō-shimashita ka. (iie) —
   3) Ototoi hatarakimashita ka. (iie) —
   4) Kinō no ban nemashita ka. (hai) —
   5) Kinō no gogo yasumimashita ka. (iie) —

Mondai

I. Rei: <u>5-ji ni</u> okimasu. — Nan-ji ni okimasu ka.
1. Kinō <u>10-ji ni</u> nemashita.
2. Asa <u>8-ji han kara</u> benkyō-shimasu.
3. Ashita wa <u>sui-yōbi</u> desu.
4. Ima <u>4-ji 15-fun</u> desu.
5. <u>9-ji kara 5-ji made</u> hatarakimasu.

II. Rei 1: Asa 6-ji ni okimasu. — Asa 6-ji ni okimasen.
Rei 2: Sore wa hon dewa arimasen. — Sore wa hon desu.
1. Watashi wa Nihon-jin desu.
2. Kesa 6-ji han ni okimashita.
3. Nihon-go no benkyō wa 8-ji kara desu.
4. Kinō no ban benkyō-shimasendeshita.
5. Ashita hatarakimasu.
6. Kore wa watashi no kagi desu.
7. Do-yōbi no gogo benkyō-shimasen.
8. Kinō no asa 7-ji ni okimashita.
9. Arora-san wa nichi-yōbi ni hatarakimasendeshita.
10. Kenshūsei wa 5-ji han made benkyō-shimasu.

III. 1. Ima nan-ji desu ka.
2. Anata wa asa nan-ji ni okimasu ka.
3. Anata wa kinō no ban nan-ji ni nemashita ka.
4. Anata wa kinō yasumimashita ka.
5. Do-yōbi no tsugi wa nan-yōbi desu ka.
6. Kenshūsei wa hiru nan-ji made yasumimasu ka.
7. Anata wa gogo nan-ji kara nan-ji made benkyō-shimasu ka.
8. Nihon-go no benkyō wa nan-ji kara desu ka.
9. Nihon-jin wa nan-yōbi kara nan-yōbi made hatarakimasu ka.
10. Anata wa kinō hatarakimashita ka.

Dai 5 Ka

Bunkei

1. Watashi wa Kyōto e ikimasu.
2. Watashi wa 4-gatsu 15-nichi ni kōjō e ikimasu.
3. Watashi wa hikōki de kuni e kaerimasu.
4. Watashi wa tomodachi to [issho ni] kimashita.

Kaiwa

Tanom: O-genki desu ka.
Lee: Hai, genki desu.
　　　 Anata wa dō desu ka.
Tanom: Watashi mo genki desu.
　　　 Anata wa ashita doko e ikimasu ka.
Lee: Doko [e] mo ikimasen.
Tanom: Dewa, watashi to issho ni Kyōto e ikimasen ka.
Lee: Sore wa ii desu ne.

Reibun

1. Anata wa kinō doko e ikimashita ka.
   —Kyōto e ikimashita.
   —Doko [e] mo ikimasendeshita.

2. Anata wa itsu Nihon e kimashita ka.
   —Sengetsu kimashita.
   Itsu kuni e kaerimasu ka.
   —9-gatsu ni kaerimasu.

3. Anata wa nan de Kyōto e ikimasu ka.
   —Shinkansen de ikimasu.

4. Lee-san wa dare to [issho ni] koko e kimashita ka.
   —Kimura-san to [issho ni] kimashita.

5. Watashi wa Echiopia kara kimashita.

6. Ōsaka kara Nagoya made jidōsha de ikimasu.

7. Anata no tanjōbi wa nan-gatsu nan-nichi desu ka.
   —6-gatsu 23-nichi desu.

Renshū A

1. Watashi wa | Indoneshia | e ikimasu.
   Tōkyō
   shokudō
   byōin
   hon-ya

   Anata wa | doko | .... ka.

2. Watashi wa | 4-gatsu | 15-nichi ni kuni e kaerimasu.
   5-gatsu
   7-gatsu
   9-gatsu
   12-gatsu

   Anata wa | nan-gatsu | nan-nichi ni | .... ka.
   | itsu |

3. Watashi wa | basu | de Tōkyō e ikimasu.
   takushii
   densha
   jidōsha
   shinkansen

   Anata wa | nan | .... ka.

4. Watashi wa | tomodachi | to [issho ni] Nihon e kimashita.
   Lee-san
   kaisha no hito

   Anata wa | dare | .... ka.

5. Watashi wa | Indo | kara kimashita.
   Mekishiko
   Iran
   Echiopia

Renshū B

1. Rei: Anata wa doko e ikimasu ka. (Tōkyō)
   —Tōkyō e ikimasu.
   (uketsuke, jimusho, toko-ya, ginkō, Tōkyō-eki, Ōsaka, Tai)

2. Rei: Anata wa nan de uchi e kaerimasu ka. (jidōsha)
   —Jidōsha de kaerimasu.
   (shinkansen, basu, takushii, chikatetsu, densha)

3. Rei: Anata wa dare to issho ni benkyō-shimasu ka. (Rao-san)
   —Rao-san to issho ni benkyō-shimasu.
   (Tanom-san, sensei, ano hito, kōjō no hito, tomodachi)

4. Rei: Tanom-san wa nan-gatsu nan-nichi ni Nihon e kimashita ka. (4/15)
   —Shi-gatsu jūgo-nichi ni kimashita.
   (8/19, 9/11, 12/23, 7/18, 4/12)

5. Rei: Ōsaka kara Kyōto made densha de ikimasu.
   1) (Ōsaka,   Tōkyō,   shinkansen)
   2) (Nihon,   Tai,   hikōki)
   3) (uchi,   kaisha,   basu)
   4) (Honkon,   Shingapōru,   fune)
   5) (Nagoya,   Kenshū Sentā,   chikatetsu)

6. Rei: Anata wa itsu kuni e kaerimasu ka. (ashita)
   —Ashita kaerimasu.
   1) (kōjō e ikimasu   :   asatte)
   2) (Nihon e kimashita   :   6-gatsu ni)
   3) (Tai e kaerimasu   :   raigetsu)
   4) (Tōkyō e ikimasu   :   nichi-yōbi ni)
   5) (Sentā e kimashita   :   kinō no ban)

7. Rei: Densha de doko e ikimasu ka. (Tōkyō)
          —Tōkyō e ikimasu.
    1) (basu   :   kōjō)
    2) (hikōki   :   Indo)
    3) (shinkansen :   Kyōto)
    4) (takushii   :   Ginza)
    5) (fune   :   Ōsutoraria)

8. Rei: Tōkyō e nan de ikimasu ka. (densha)
          —Densha de ikimasu.
    1) (kaisha   :   basu)
    2) (Ginza   :   takushii)
    3) (Ōsaka   :   shinkansen)
    4) (ginkō   :   *aruite)
    5) (Amerika   :   hikōki)

9. Rei: Anata wa dare to issho ni kaisha e ikimashita ka. (Rao-san)
          —Rao-san to issho ni ikimashita.
    1) (kōjō   :   Arora-san)
    2) (depāto   :   tomodachi)
    3) (hon-ya   :   sensei)
    4) (Tōkyō   :   Kimura-san)
    5) (byōin   :   *hitori de)

10. Rei: Anata wa ashita doko e ikimasu ka. (Yokohama)
          —Yokohama e ikimasu.
    1) (konban   :   toko-ya)
    2) (kesa   :   byōin)
    3) (raishū   :   Ōsaka)
    4) (ashita   :   *doko mo)
    5) (kinō   :   *doko mo)

11. Rei: ikimasu ....ikimasu
          Tōkyō e ....Tōkyō e ikimasu
          shinkansen de ......shinkansen de Tōkyō e ikimasu
          ashita ......Ashita shinkansen de Tōkyō e ikimasu.
    1) ikimashita   2) kaerimasu   3) kimashita
       shokudō e   kuni e   Nihon e
       9-ji ni   hikōki de   Rao-san to
       kesa   raigetsu   nichi-yōbi ni

— 32 —

Mondai

I. 1. (   ) to issho ni benkyō-shimasu ka.
     —Ali-san to benkyō-shimasu.

   2. Ano hito wa (   ) desu ka.
     —Tanom-san desu.

   3. Tanom-san no o-kuni wa (   ) desu ka.
     —Tai desu.

   4. Ashita (   ) e ikimasu ka.
     —Doko e mo ikimasen.

   5. Kyō wa (   ) (   ) desu ka.
     —2-gatsu 18-nichi desu.

   6. Abebe-san wa (   ) Nihon e kimashita ka.
     —4-gatsu 15-nichi ni kimashita.

   7. Anata wa (   ) de kuni e kaerimasu ka.
     —Hikōki de kaerimasu.

   8. Anata wa asa (   ) ni shokudō e ikimasu ka.
     —7-ji han ni ikimasu.

   9. Anata wa doko e ikimasu ka.
     —(   ) ikimasen.

  10. Tanaka-san wa (   ) no sensei desu ka.
     —Nihon-go no sensei desu.

II. Konnichiwa. Watashi [   ] Slamet desu. Indoneshia [   ] kimashita. Sengetsu hikōki [   ] kimashita. Tanom-san wa watashi [   ] tomodachi desu. Tanom-san [   ] kuni wa Tai desu. Kinō watashi wa Tanom-san [   ] issho ni depāto [   ] ikimashita. Chikatetsu [   ] ikimashita. Ban 11-ji han [   ] takushii [   ] Sentā [   ] kaerimashita.

III. 1. Anata wa nan de Nihon e kimashita ka.
    2. Dare to issho ni Nihon e kimashita ka.
    3. Itsu Nihon e kimashita ka.
    4. Anata wa nichi-yōbi ni doko e ikimasu ka.
    5. Kinō doko e ikimashita ka.
    6. Kyō wa nan-gatsu nan-nichi desu ka.
    7. Anata no tanjōbi wa itsu desu ka.

Dai 6 Ka

Bunkei

1. Watashi wa gohan o tabemasu.
2. Watashi wa Ōsaka de jisshū-shimasu.
3. Issho ni rekōdo o kikimashō.

Kaiwa

Cortez: Kinō nani o shimashita ka.
Slamet: Asa Nihon-go o benkyō-shimashita.
           Gogo tomodachi to Ginza e ikimashita.
Cortez: Koko kara Ginza made donokurai kakarimasu ka.
Slamet: Takushii de 30-pun desu.
Cortez: Sō desu ka.
           Ginza de nani o shimashita ka.
Slamet: Depāto de kono kamera o kaimashita.

Reibun

1. Anata wa tabako o suimasu ka.
    —Hai, suimasu.
    —Iie, suimasen.

2. Anata wa maiasa nani o tabemasu ka.
    —Pan to tamago o tabemasu.
    —Nani mo tabemasen. Gyūnyū o nomimasu.

3. Anata wa doko de shashin o torimasu ka.
    —Niwa de torimasu.

4. Anata wa kinō no ban nani o shimashita ka.
    —Shokudō de terebi o mimashita.
    Ashita nani o shimasu ka.
    —Kyōto e ikimasu.

5. Issho ni ocha o nomimasen ka.
    —Hai, nomimashō.

Renshū A

1. Watashi wa | gohan | o tabemasu.
pan
ringo
niku
yasai

   Anata wa | nani | .... ka.

2. Watashi wa nani mo | tabemasen.
nomimasen.
kaimasendeshita.
shimasendeshita.

3. Watashi wa | kyōshitsu | de shashin o torimashita.
niwa
kōjō
heya
Nara

   Anata wa | doko | .... ka.

4.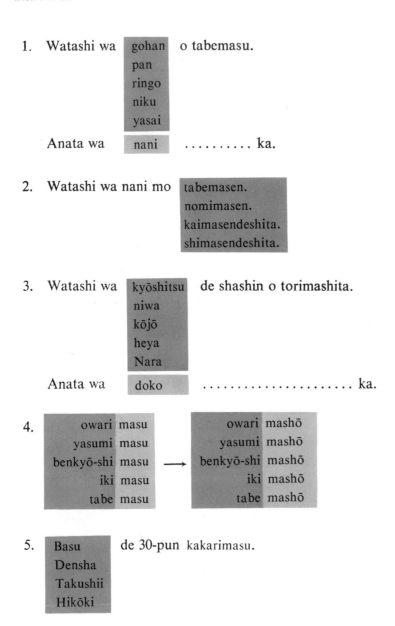

owari masu ⟶ owari mashō
yasumi masu ⟶ yasumi mashō
benkyō-shi masu ⟶ benkyō-shi mashō
iki masu ⟶ iki mashō
tabe masu ⟶ tabe mashō

5. | Basu | de 30-pun kakarimasu.
Densha
Takushii
Hikōki

Renshū B

1. 1) Rei: Watashi wa <u>gohan</u> o tabemasu.
      (tamago, pan, ringo, niku, yasai, sakana)
   2) Rei: Watashi wa <u>ocha</u> o nomimasu.
      (mizu, kōcha, biiru, gyūnyū, kōhii, jūsu)
   3) Rei: Watashi wa <u>hon</u> o yomimasu.
      (shinbun, tegami, zasshi, Nihon-go no hon)

2. Chāto 5
   1) Gohan o tabemasu.
   2) Hana o kaimasu.
   3) Tabako o suimasu.
   4) Kōhii o nomimasu.
   5) Shashin o torimasu.
   6) Rekōdo o kikimasu.
   7) Hon o yomimasu.
   8) Tegami o kakimasu.
   9) Terebi o mimasu.
   10) Nihon-go o benkyō-shimasu.

3. Rei: Anata wa nani o <u>tabemasu</u> ka. (ringo)
        —Ringo o tabemasu.

1) (nomimasu	:	biiru)
2) (mimasu	:	Nihon no eiga)
3) (kikimasu	:	rekōdo)
4) (yomimasu	:	Ei-go no shinbun)
5) (kaimasu	:	*nani mo)

4. Chāto 5
   1) Rei: (shokudō) — <u>Shokudō</u> de gohan o tabemasu.
   2) (depāto)   6) (heya)
   3) (robii)   7) (uchi)
   4) (heya)   8) (jimusho)
   5) (niwa)   9) (robii)
                                 10) (kyōshitsu)

5. Rei: Doko de <u>kutsu</u> o kaimashita ka.
   (nekutai, kippu, shatsu, kudamono, kusuri, kitte to fūtō)

6. Chāto 5

   1) Rei: Anata wa doko de <u>gohan o tabemasu</u> ka. (shokudō)
      —<u>Shokudō</u> de tabemasu.

   2) (hana o kaimasu   :   hana-ya)
   3) (tabako o suimasu   :   robii)
   4) (kōhii o nomimasu   :   heya)
   5) (shashin o torimasu   :   niwa)
   6) (rekōdo o kikimasu   :   heya)

7. Rei: Anata wa <u>Sentā</u> de nani o shimasu ka.
        (Nihon-go o benkyō-shimasu) — <u>Nihon-go o benkyō-shimasu</u>.

   1) (niwa   :   shashin o torimasu)
   2) (kyōshitsu   :   kōgi o kikimasu)
   3) (heya   :   benkyō-shimasu)
   4) (koko   :   tegami o kakimasu)
   5) (Nagoya   :   jisshū-shimasu)

8. Rei: Anata wa nani o tabemasu ka. (ringo)
        —<u>Ringo</u> o tabemasu.

   1) Anata wa nani o nomimasu ka. (ocha) —
   2) Anata wa nani o kaimasu ka. (nani mo) —
   3) Anata wa tegami o kakimasu ka. (iie) —
   4) Anata wa nani o benkyō-shimashita ka. (nani mo) —
   5) Anata wa shinbun o yomimashita ka. (hai) —

9. Rei: (Tōkyō e ikimasu)
        Tōkyō e ikimasen ka. — Hai, ikimashō.

   1) (Sentā e kaerimasu)   4) (pinpon-shimasu)
   2) (robii de yasumimasu)   5) (terebi o mimasu)
   3) (issho ni benkyō-shimasu)   6) (rajio o kikimasu)

10. Rei: <u>Basu</u> de donokurai kakarimasu ka. (30-pun)
         —<u>30-pun</u> kakarimasu.

    1) (densha   :   15-fun)
    2) (takushii   :   10-pun)
    3) (shinkansen   :   3-jikan)
    4) (hikōki   :   4-jikan han)
    5) (aruite*   :   1-jikan)

Mondai

I. Watashi ☐ Indo ☐ Rao desu. Sentā ☐ mainichi Nihon-go ☐ benkyō-shimasu. Nihon-go ☐ benkyō wa asa 9-ji ☐ 12-ji ☐ desu. Soshite shokudō ☐ hirugohan ☐ tabemasu. Gogo 2-ji ☐ kōgi ☐ kikimasu. Kinō 1-ji ☐ basu ☐ kōjō ☐ ikimashita.

II. Rei: <u>Mizu o</u> nomimasu — Nani o nomimasu ka.
1. <u>Kōjō de</u> sono shashin o torimashita.
2. Nihon de <u>kikai o</u> jisshū-shimasu.
3. <u>Kinō</u> kamera o kaimashita.
4. Hikōki de <u>20-jikan</u> kakarimasu.
5. <u>Ashita no gogo</u> kōgi o kikimasu.
6. Tōkyō e <u>shinkansen de</u> ikimashita.
7. <u>Uketsuke de</u> kitte o kaimashita.
8. Maiasa <u>pan to tamago</u> o tabemasu.
9. <u>Nagoya no kōjō de</u> jisshū-shimasu.
10. Kesa <u>nani mo</u> nomimasendeshita.

III. 1. Anata wa tabako o suimasu ka.
2. Anata wa o-sake o nomimasu ka.
3. Anata wa kesa gyūnyū o nomimashita ka.
4. Anata wa doko de Nihon-go o benkyō-shimasu ka.
5. Uketsuke de nani o kaimasu ka.
6. Anata wa doko de jisshū-shimasu ka.
7. Ashita no gogo nani o shimasu ka.
8. Anata no kuni kara Nihon made hikōki de donokurai kakarimasu ka.
9. Anata wa mainichi nani o shimasu ka.
10. Anata wa kesa nan-ji ni asagohan o tabemashita ka.

— 39 —

Dai 7 Ka

Bunkei

1. Nihon-jin wa hashi de gohan o tabemasu.
2. Watashi wa Nihon-go de repōto o kakimasu.
3. Watashi wa tomodachi ni denwa o kakemasu.
4. Watashi wa Tanaka-san ni (kara) Nihon-go o naraimashita.

Kaiwa

Slamet: Chotto sumimasen.
Tanaka: Hai, nan desu ka.
Slamet: Kono nimotsu wa ea-mēru de ikura desu ka.
Tanaka: Doko ni okurimasu ka.
Slamet: Indoneshia no Jakaruta desu.
Tanaka: 1-kiro desu ne.
           600-en desu.
Slamet: Raishū tsukimasu ka.
Tanaka: Ē, daijōbu desu.
Slamet: Dewa, onegai-shimasu.

Reibun

1. Nan de jidōsha o shūri-shimasu ka.
    —Doraibā to supana de shūri-shimasu.

2. "Good night" wa Nihon-go de nan desu ka.
    —"Oyasuminasai" desu.

3. Anata wa dare ni sono hon o agemasu ka.
    —Tanom-san ni agemasu.

4. Anata wa Slamet-san ni nani o moraimashita ka.
    —Tokei o moraimashita.

5. Kono hon o yomimashita ka.
    —Hai, mō yomimashita.
    —Iie, mada yomimasen.

Renshū A

1. Watashi wa | hashi / supūn / fōku to naifu / te | de gohan o tabemasu.

   Anata wa | nan | . . . . ka.

2. Watashi wa | Nihon-go / Ei-go / Chūgoku-go / Supein-go | de repōto o kakimasu.

3. Kore wa | Nihon-go / Arabia-go / Indoneshia-go / Tai-go | de nan desu ka.

4. Watashi wa | tomodachi / Lee-san / koibito / kaisha / uchi | ni denwa o kakemasu.

   Anata wa | dare, doko | . . . . ka.

5. Watashi wa Tanaka-san ni | tokei / rekōdo / kitte / shashin / hon | o moraimashita.

   Anata wa . . . . | nani | . . . . ka.

Renshū B

1. 1) Rei: <u>Nihon-jin</u> wa nan de gohan o tabemasu ka.
   (anata, Echiopia-jin, Indo-jin, Arabia-jin, Tai-jin)
   2) Rei: Nan de <u>jidōsha</u> o shūri-shimasu ka.
   (kamera, rajio, terebi, tokei, kutsu)

2. Rei: Anata wa nan de <u>gohan o tabemasu</u> ka. (hashi)
   —<u>Hashi</u> de tabemasu.
   1) (gohan o tabemasu   :   fōku to supūn)
   2) (tegami o kakimasu   :   bōrupen)
   3) (terebi o shūri-shimasu   :   doraibā to supana)
   4) (ringo o kirimasu   :   naifu)

3. Rei: "Good morning" wa Nihon-go de nan desu ka.
   —[Nihon-go de] "Ohayō gozaimasu" desu.
   1) (Thank you   :   arigatō gozaimasu)
   2) (Good by   :   sayōnara)
   3) (friend   :   tomodachi)
   4) (photograph   :   shashin)
   5) (flower   :   hana)

4. 1) Rei: Watashi wa <u>tomodachi</u> ni tegami o kakimashita.
   (okāsan, otōsan, oniisan, onēsan, koibito, kodomo)
   2) Rei: Watashi wa Lee-san ni <u>okane</u> o kashimashita.
   (bōrupen, penchi, naifu, kamera, rekōdo, jisho)

5. Rei: Watashi wa <u>Tanaka-san</u> ni <u>Nihon-go</u> o naraimashita.
   1) (Cortez-san, Supein-go)
   2) (Tanom-san, Tai-go)
   3) (Slamet-san, Indoneshia-go)
   4) (Lee-san, Chūgoku-go)
   5) (Ali-san, Arabia-go)

6. Rei: Anata wa <u>okusan</u> ni nani o agemasu ka. (hon)
        —<u>Hon</u> o agemasu.
    1) (kodomo   :   kutsu)
    2) (koibito   :   hana)
    3) (tomodachi   :   jisho)
    4) (Tanom-san   :   kitte)
    5) (ano hito   :   katarogu)

7. Chāto 1

    1) Rei: Anata wa dare ni <u>tegami</u> o kakimashita ka.
            (Tanom-san) — <u>Tanom-san</u> ni kakimashita.
    2) (Nihon-go o oshiemasu   :   Abebe-san)
    3) (jisho o kashimasu   :   Cortez-san)
    4) (hana o agemasu   :   Kimura-san)
    5) (denwa o kakemasu   :   Lee-san)
    6) (nimotsu o okurimasu   :   Rao-san)

8. Chāto 3

    1) Rei: Anata wa <u>ano hito</u> ni nani o moraimashita ka. (hon)
            —<u>Hon</u> o moraimashita.
    2) (sensei   :   enpitsu)
    3) (otōsan   :   kaban)
    4) (tomodachi   :   matchi)
    5) (koibito   :   rajio)
    6) (kaisha no hito   :   terebi)

9. Rei 1: Mō Tōkyō e ikimashita ka. (hai) — Hai, mō ikimashita.
   Rei 2: Mō Ōsaka e ikimashita ka. (iie) — Iie, mada ikimasen.
    1) Mō asagohan o tabemashita ka. (hai) —
    2) Mō nimotsu o okurimashita ka. (iie) —
    3) Mō Nihon no eiga o mimashita ka. (hai) —
    4) Mō kaisha ni denwa o kakemashita ka. (iie) —
    5) Mō benkyō wa owarimashita ka. (iie) —

Mondai

I. 1. Nihon-jin ☐ hashi ☐ gohan ☐ tabemasu.
   2. Anata wa dare ☐ sono hon o agemasu ka.
   3. "Arigatō" wa Ei-go ☐ nan desu ka.
   4. Kimura-san wa 7-ji ☐ tomodachi ☐ denwa o kakemasu.
   5. Nan ☐ jidōsha o shūri-shimasu ka.
   6. Kenshūsei wa sensei ☐ Nihon-go ☐ naraimasu.
   7. Watashi-tachi wa kyōshitsu ☐ kōgi o kikimasu.
   8. Arora-san wa 9-gatsu 11-nichi ☐ Nihon e kimashita.
   9. Doraibā ☐ penchi ☐ kikai ☐ shūri-shimasu.
   10. Issho ni shokudō ☐ ikimashō.

II. Rei: <u>Tomodachi ni</u> tegami o kakimasu.
   　　　　—Dare ni tegami o kakimasu ka.
   1. Ali-san ni <u>kitte</u> o moraimashita.
   2. <u>Kaisha ni</u> denwa o kakemashita.
   3. <u>Naifu de</u> kami o kirimasu.
   4. "Good evening" wa Nihon-go de "<u>Konbanwa</u>" desu.
   5. Nimotsu wa <u>raishū</u> tsukimasu.

III. 1. Anata wa mainichi tegami o kakimasu ka.
   2. Dare ni tegami o kakimasu ka.
   3. "Konnichiwa" wa Ei-go de nan desu ka.
   4. Anata wa nan de gohan o tabemasu ka.
   5. Anata wa dare ni Nihon-go o naraimasu ka.
   6. Anata wa tanjōbi ni nani o moraimashita ka.
   7. Kyō kaisha ni denwa o kakemasu ka.
   8. Sensei wa kenshūsei ni nani o oshiemasu ka.
   9. Anata wa mō bangohan o tabemashita ka.
   10. Anata no kuni made tegami wa ea-mēru de ikura desu ka.

Dai 8 Ka

Bunkei

1. Sakura wa kireina hana desu.
2. Sakura wa kirei desu.
3. Sakura wa kirei dewa arimasen.
4. Kore wa ōkii kaban desu.
5. Kore wa ōkii desu.
6. Kore wa ōkikunai desu.
      (ōkiku arimasen.)

Kaiwa

Ali: Tadaima.
Kimura: Okaerinasai.
           Doko e ikimashita ka.
Ali: Tanom-san no uchi e ikimashita.
Kimura: Sō desu ka.
           Donna uchi desu ka.
Ali: Chiisai desu ga, atarashii uchi desu.
           Tanom-san no okusan ni aimashita.
Kimura: Okusan wa donna hito desu ka.
Ali: Kireina hito desu, soshite taihen shinsetsu desu.

Reibun

1. Tanaka-san wa shinsetsu desu ka.
   —Hai, shinsetsu desu.
   —Iie, shinsetsu dewa arimasen.

2. Sono kamera wa ii desu ka.
   —Hai, taihen ii desu.
   —Iie, amari yokunai desu.

3. Nara wa donna machi desu ka.
   —Shizukana machi desu.

4. Nihon no tabemono wa dō desu ka.
   —Oishii desu.

5. Anata no kuni wa ima atsui desu ka, samui desu ka.
   —Taihen atsui desu.

6. Shiken wa muzukashii desu ka.
   —Iie, muzukashikunai desu, yasashii desu.

7. Ano akai kaban wa dare no desu ka.
   —Tanaka-san no desu.

Renshū A

1. Arora-san wa

kirei	na
genki	na
shinsetsu	na
yūmei	na

hito desu.

2. Kimura-san wa

kirei
genki
shinsetsu
yūmei

desu.

3. Kore wa

ōki	i
i	i
atarashi	i
shiro	i

kaban desu.

4. Kore wa

chiisa	i
waru	i
furu	i
aka	i

desu.

5.

kirei
genki
shizuka
hansamu

desu $\longrightarrow$

kirei
genki
shizuka
hansamu

dewa arimasen

6.

ōki	i
i	i
atsu	i
omoshiro	i

desu $\longrightarrow$

ōki	kunai
yo	kunai
atsu	kunai
omoshiro	kunai

desu

Renshū B

1. Chāto 3

   1) Rei: <u>Hon</u> o kaimashita. (takai) — <u>Takai</u> hon o kaimashita.

   2) (ii)

   3) (kuroi)

   4) (kireina)

   5) (chiisai)

   6) (ōkii)

2. Chāto 3

   7) Rei: Kore wa <u>zasshi</u> desu. (omoshiroi)

      —Kore wa <u>omoshiroi</u> zasshi desu.

   8) (ii)

   9) (yūmeina)

   10) (atarashii)

   11) (yasui)

   12) (furui)

3. Rei 1: Tanaka-san wa kireina hito desu.

   　　　　—Tanaka-san wa kirei desu.

   Rei 2: Tanaka-san wa omoshiroi hito desu.

   　　　　—Tanaka-san wa omoshiroi desu.

   1) Ali-san wa shinsetsuna hito desu. —

   2) Kore wa ii kamera desu. —

   3) Tai wa atsui kuni desu. —

   4) Tai wa kireina kuni desu. —

   5) Kyōto wa yūmeina machi desu. —

   6) Kyōto wa furui machi desu. —

   7) Nara wa shizukana tokoro desu. —

   8) Are wa oishii tabemono desu. —

4. Rei: kore wa kamera desu, ii desu

   　　　—Kore wa ii kamera desu.

   1) are wa terebi desu, atarashii desu —

   2) Tanaka-san wa sensei desu, hansamu desu —

   3) Indo wa kuni desu, furui desu —

   4) Kyōto wa machi desu, yūmei desu —

   5) kore wa kitte desu, kirei desu —

   6) sore wa shiken desu, yasashii desu —

   7) kore wa gyūnyū desu, tsumetai desu —

   8) Nara wa machi desu, shizuka desu —

5. Rei 1: Ano hito wa kirei desu.
      —Ano hito wa kirei dewa arimasen.
   Rei 2: Kono hon wa omoshiroi desu.
      —Kono hon wa omoshirokunai desu.

   1) Nihon-jin wa shinsetsu desu. —
   2) Kyō wa atsui desu. —
   3) Kenshū Sentā wa shizuka desu. —
   4) Nihon-go wa muzukashii desu. —
   5) Watashi no kuni wa samui desu. —
   6) Ano sensei wa genki desu. —
   7) Kono pen wa ii desu. —
   8) Shinkansen wa yūmei desu. —

6. Rei 1: Tōkyō wa ōkii desu ka. (hai)
      —Hai, taihen ōkii desu.
   Rei 2: Sentā wa ōkii desu ka. (iie)
      —Iie, amari ōkikunai desu.

   1) Kono ringo wa oishii desu ka. (hai) —
   2) Kyō wa samui desu ka. (iie) —
   3) Ano sensei wa shinsetsu desu ka. (iie) —
   4) Lee-san wa genki desu ka. (hai) —
   5) Ano hon wa ii desu ka. (iie) —
   6) Shiken wa muzukashii desu ka. (hai) —
   7) Ano hito wa yūmei desu ka. (hai) —
   8) Sono mizu wa tsumetai desu ka. (iie) —

7. Rei: Echiopia wa donna kuni desu ka. (furui desu)
      —Furui kuni desu.

   1) (Arora-san, hito   :   shinsetsu desu)
   2) (Fujisan, yama   :   takai desu)
   3) (Nara, machi   :   shizuka desu)
   4) (Tanaka-san, sensei   :   omoshiroi desu)
   5) (Hokkaidō, tokoro   :   taihen samui desu)

NIHONGO NO KISO I

—Mondai no Kotae—

KAIGAI GIJUTSUSHA KENSHŪ KYŌKAI

I. 1. Lee-san
    2. sensei
    3. Indoneshia-jin
    4. Mekishiko-jin
    5. kenshūsei
    6. Indo-jin
    7. dare (donata)
    8. Ali-san
    9. Nihon-jin
    10. Nihon-jin

II. 1. Iie, watashi wa Nihon-jin dewa arimasen.
    2. [Watashi wa] kenshūsei desu.
    3. Iie, watashi wa Echiopia-jin dewa arimasen.
    4. Iie, watashi wa Lee dewa arimasen.
    5. [Watashi wa] Slamet desu.

I. 1. hon
 2. nan
 3. dare
 4. Lee-san
 5. anata
 6. pen
 7. nan
 8. dare
 9. nan-sai (o-ikutsu)
 10. dare no

II. 1. Are wa nan desu ka.
 2. Sore wa dare no kagi desu ka.
 3. Kono jisho wa anata no desu.

III. 1. [Watashi no namae wa] Slamet desu.
 2. [Watashi wa] 21 [-sai] desu.
 3. [Watashi no senmon wa] terebi desu.
 4. Hai, sō desu.
 5. [Watashi no sensei wa] Tanaka-san desu.

I. 1. Tanom-san wa doko desu ka.
    2. Otearai wa dochira desu ka.
    3. Kore wa ikura desu ka.
    4. Sore wa nan no hon desu ka.
    5. Anata no o-kuni wa dochira (doko) desu ka.
    6. Cortez-san no kaisha wa dochira (doko) desu ka.
    7. Sore wa doko no tokei desu ka.
    8. Anata no kaban wa doko desu ka.

II. 1. koko
    2. Sono, watashi no
    3. Nihon-jin
    4. to, Soshite

III. 1. [Watashi no kuni wa] Indoneshia desu.
     2. [Watashi no kaisha wa] Yokohama-denki desu.
     3. [Watashi no tokei wa] 2-man-en desu.
     4. [Watashi no heya no kagi wa] uketsuke desu.
     5. [Watashi no kaisha wa] denki no kaisha desu.

I. 1. Kinō nan-ji ni nemashita ka.
   2. Asa nan-ji kara benkyō-shimasu ka.
   3. Ashita wa nan-yōbi desu ka.
   4. Ima nan-ji desu ka.
   5. Nan-ji kara nan-ji made hatarakimasu ka.

II. 1. Watashi wa Nihon-jin dewa arimasen.
    2. Kesa 6-ji han ni okimasendeshita.
    3. Nihon-go no benkyō wa 8-ji kara dewa arimasen.
    4. Kinō no ban benkyō-shimashita.
    5. Ashita hatarakimasen.
    6. Kore wa watashi no kagi dewa arimasen.
    7. Do-yōbi no gogo benkyō-shimasu.
    8. Kinō no asa 7-ji ni okimasendeshita.
    9. Arora-san wa nichi-yōbi ni hatarakimashita.
   10. Kenshūsei wa 5-ji han made benkyō-shimasen.

III. 1. [Ima] 10-ji han desu.
     2. [Watashi wa asa] 6-ji han ni okimasu.
     3. [Watashi wa kinō no ban] 11-ji ni nemashita.
     4. Iie, [watashi wa kinō] yasumimasendeshita.
     5. [Do-yōbi no tsugi wa] nichi-yōbi desu.
     6. [Kenshūsei wa hiru] 2-ji made yasumimasu.
     7. [Watashi wa gogo] 2-ji kara 5-ji made benkyō-shimasu.
     8. [Nihon-go no benkyō wa] 9-ji kara desu.
     9. [Nihon-jin wa] getsu-yōbi kara do-yōbi made hatarakimasu.
    10. Iie, [watashi wa kinō] hatarakimasendeshita.

I. 1. Dare
    2. dare
    3. dochira (doko)
    4. doko
    5. nan-gatsu, nan-nichi
    6. itsu
    7. nan
    8. nan-ji
    9. Doko e mo
   10. nan

II. wa, kara, de, no, no, to, e, de, ni, de, e

III. 1. Hikōki de kimashita.
     2. Tomodachi to kimashita.
     3. Sengetsu kimashita.
     4. Depāto e ikimasu. (Doko mo ikimasen.)
     5. Ginkō e ikimashita. (Doko mo ikimasendeshita.)
     6. 9-gatsu 14-ka desu.
     7. 5-gatsu 16-nichi desu.

I.   wa, no, de, o, no, kara, made, de, o, kara, o, ni, de, e

II.   1.   Doko de sono shashin o torimashita ka.
  2.   Nihon de nani o jisshū-shimasu ka.
  3.   Itsu kamera o kaimashita ka.
  4.   Hikōki de donokurai (nan-jikan) kakarimasu ka.
  5.   Itsu kōgi o kikimasu ka.
  6.   Tōkyō e nan de ikimashita ka.
  7.   Doko de kitte o kaimashita ka.
  8.   Maiasa nani o tabemasu ka.
  9.   Doko [no kōjō] de jisshū-shimasu ka.
  10.   Kesa nani o nomimashita ka.

III.   1.   Iie, suimasen.
  2.   Hai, nomimasu.
  3.   Hai, nomimashita.
  4.   Kyōshitsu de benkyō-shimasu.
  5.   Kitte to fūtō o kaimasu.
  6.   Yokohama de jisshū-shimasu.
  7.   Kōjō e ikimasu.
  8.   8-jikan kakarimasu.
  9.   Nihon-go o benkyō-shimasu.
  10.   7-ji han ni tabemashita.

I. 1. wa, de, o   2. ni
   3. de   4. ni, ni
   5. de   6. ni, o
   7. de   8. ni
   9. to, de, o   10. e

II. 1. Ali-san ni nani o moraimashita ka.
    2. Doko ni denwa o kakemashita ka.
    3. Nan de kami o kirimasu ka.
    4. "Good evening" wa Nihon-go de nan desu ka.
    5. Nimotsu wa itsu tsukimasu ka.

III. 1. Iie, mainichi kakimasen.
     2. Okāsan ni kakimasu.
     3. "Good afternoon" desu.
     4. Supūn to fōku de tabemasu.
     5. Tanaka-san ni naraimasu.
     6. Nekutai o moraimashita.
     7. Iie, kakemasen.
     8. Nihon-go o oshiemasu.
     9. Iie, mada tabemasen.
     10. 60-en desu.

I.   1. kireina, kirei
     2. omoshiroi, omoshiroi
     3. shizukana, shizuka
     4. yūmeina, yūmei
     5. furui, furuku

II. 1. Kono kōhii wa tsumetakunai desu.
     2. Sono pen wa warukunai desu.
     3. Watashi no kutsu wa atarashikunai desu.
     4. Kyō wa atsukunai desu.
     5. Kono shiken wa yasashikunai desu.

III. 1. Hai, omoshiroi desu.
     2. Taihen atsui kuni desu.
     3. Hai, ii desu.
     4. Oishii desu.
     5. Chiisai heya desu.
     6. Shinsetsuna hito desu.
     7. Iie, amari oishikunai desu.
     8. Shizukana tokoro desu.
     9. Takai desu.
    10. Iie, yasukunai desu, takai desu.

I. 1. Arora-san wa tenisu ga jōzu dewa arimasen.
    2. Watashi wa kanji ga wakarimasen.
    3. Watashi wa tabako ga suki dewa arimasen.
    4. Watashi wa kodomo ga arimasen.
    5. Kono bōrupen wa watashi no dewa arimasen.

II. 1. atama ga itai desu
    2. Benkyō-shimasendeshita
    3. byōin e ikimasendeshita
    4. Kaze o hikimashita
    5. kusuri o nomimasu

III. 1. Iie, amari suki dewa arimasen.
    2. Jūsu ga suki desu.
    3. Kirai desu.
    4. Iie, amari jōzu dewa arimasen.
    5. Hai, wakarimasu.
    6. Hai, wakarimasu.
    7. 25,000-en arimasu.
    8. Iie, wakarimasen.
    9. Iie, arimasen.
    10. Futtobōru ga suki desu.

Dai 10 ka   (63 pēji)

I. 1. arimasu
    2. imasen
    3. arimasu
    4. imasu
    5. imasu

II. 1. ×
    2. ○
    3. ×
    4. ×
    5. ○

III. 1. Kyōshitsu ni imasu.
     2. Hon ya pen nado ga arimasu.
     3. Doa no migi ni arimasu.
     4. Tōkyō ni arimasu.
     5. Hai, takusan imasu.
     6. Tsukue no ue ni arimasu.
     7. Tai ya Firipin no hito ga imasu.
     8. Dare mo imasen.
     9. Indoneshia no Jakaruta ni imasu.
    10. Iie, arimasen.

I. 1. Kenshūsei ga hitori imasu.
   2. Jidōsha ga 5-dai arimasu.
   3. Ringo o futatsu tabemashita.
   4. Kikai ga 50-dai arimasu.
   5. Kami o 3-mai moraimashita.

II. 1. 2-mai arimasu.
   2. 4-nin desu.
   3. Yottsu arimasu.
   4. 300-en desu.
   5. 4-kagetsu han imasu.

III. 1. 3-jikan benkyō-shimasu.
   2. 2-kai kakimasu.
   3. 5-shūkan naraimasu.
   4. 6-kagetsu jisshū-shimasu.
   5. 6-nin arimasu.
   6. 15-fun desu.
   7. Yottsu arimasu.
   8. 40-nin imasu.
   9. Daitai 4-shūkan desu.
   10. Nanoka desu.

I. 1. warui   6. takai
   2. atsui   7. suki
   3. yasashii   8. wakai
   4. hima(na)   9. tōi
   5. heta   10. hayai

II. 1. dochira   2. nan   3. dore
    4. doko   5. nani   6. dare

III. 1. Kōhii no hō ga suki desu.
     2. Toriniku ga ichiban suki desu.
     3. Lee-san ga ichiban toshi-ue desu.
     4. Nichi-yōbi no hō ga hima desu.
     5. Ryokō ga ichiban omoshiroi desu.
     6. 1-gatsu ga ichiban samui desu.
     7. Iie, ame dewa arimasendeshita.
     8. Hai, muzukashikatta desu.
     9. Iie, atsukunai desu. (Iie, Indo yori samui desu.)
     10. Toriniku-ryōri desu.

I. 1. Doko e ikitai desu ka.
    2. Itsu ano hito ni aitai desu ka.
    3. Nihon de nani o shitai desu ka.
    4. Dare to kekkon-shitai desu ka.
    5. Doko e kitte o kai ni ikimasu ka.
    6. Donna jidōsha ga hoshii desu ka.
    7. Depāto e nani o kai ni ikimasu ka.
    8. Nani ga hoshii desu ka.

II. no, wa, kara, o, no, to, ga, wa, ga, o, no, e, o, ni

III. 1. Terebi no jisshū ni kimashita.
     2. Chiisai kamera ga hoshii desu.
     3. Koibito ni ichiban aitai desu.
     4. Ryōhō hoshii desu.
     5. Konpyūtā no kōjō o kengaku-shitai desu.
     6. Tōkyō e ikitai desu.
     7. Okane o kae ni ikimasu.
     8. Sukiyaki ga tabetai desu.
     9. Tōkyō e asobi ni ikitai desu.
    10. Senshū ikimashita.

I. 1. de, o, mite kudasai
   2. ni, okite kudasai
   3. o, totte kudasai
   4. ni, o, yonde kudasai
   5. to, de, o, shūri-shite kudasai
   6. o, ni, okutte kudasai
   7. ni, o, kashite kudasai
   8. o, oboete kudasai
   9. ni, haitte kudasai
   10. no, o, oshiete kudasai

II. 1. oshiete
   2. Arora-san ga mada kimasen
   3. nete
   4. Okane ga zenzen arimasen
   5. misete

III. 1. Iie, sutte imasen.
   2. Watashi no heya de benkyō-shite imasu.
   3. Nihon-go o benkyō-shite imasu.
   4. Iie, futte imasen.
   5. Iie, kiite imasen.

I. 1. yonde   2. nomi   3. mi
    4. hataraki   5. totte   6. jisshū
    7. sutte   8. tabete   9. hanashi
    10. tetsudatte

II. 1. Hai, totte kudasai.
     2. Hai, itte kudasai.
     3. Hai, kaite kudasai.
     4. Dare o yobimashō ka.
     5. Nan de kakimashō ka.
     6. Ringo o ikutsu kaimashō ka.

III. 1. Iie, ikemasen.
     2. Indoneshia no Jakaruta ni sunde imasu.
     3. Hai, sukoshi ii desu.
     4. Hai, shitte imasu. (Iie, shirimasen.)
     5. Iie, motte imasen.
     6. 20-sai kara sutte mo ii desu.
     7. "Sari" o kite imasu.
     8. Iie, mada kekkon-shite imasen.
     9. Kitte ya matchi o utte imasu.
     10. Terebi-kōjō de hataraite imasu.

I. 1. itte, atte
    2. tabete, nonde
    3. wakakute, kirei de
    4. karukute, kantan de
    5. nichi-yōbi de

II. 1. ga, o   2. ga, o
     3. e   4. ni, ga
     5. de, o

III. 1. Terebi o mite, shinbun o yonde, sukoshi yasumimasu.
      2. Nihon-go o benkyō-shite kara, kazoku ni tegami o kakimasu.
      3. Jakaruta no terebi-kōjō de hatarakimasu.
      4. Wakakute, omoshiroi hito desu.
      5. Jidōsha ga ōkute, tabemono ga takai desu.
      6. 2-jikan yasumimasu.
      7. Ginza ya Yokohama e ikimashita.
      8. Kōgi o kikimasu.
      9. Bangohan o tabete kara, benkyō-shimasu.
      10. 5-shūkan naratte kara, jisshū-shimasu.

I.   1.   hataraite mo ii desu
     2.   harawanakute mo ii desu
     3.   shinpai-shinai de kudasai
     4.   benkyō-shinakereba narimasen

II.   1.   totte, totte, tora
      2.   sutte, suwa, sui

III.   1.   8-ji ni okinakereba narimasen.
       2.   Muika hatarakanakereba narimasen.
       3.   Hai, dasanakereba narimasen.
       4.   Iie, [mainichi] sentaku-shinakute mo ii desu.
       5.   6-kagetsu jisshū-shinakereba narimasen.
       6.   Yokohama no kōjō de jisshū-shinakereba narimasen.
       7.   Rainen no 3-gatsu ni kaeranakereba narimasen.
       8.   60-en no kitte o kawanakereba narimasen.
       9.   Jakaruta no terebi-kōjō de hatarakanakereba narimasen.
      10.   Pasupōto ya okane o motte ikanakereba narimasen.

I. 1. Neru   2. Benkyō-shite   3. iku
    4. Dekakeru   5. kaette

II. 1. asonde, asoba, asonde
    2. hanasu, hanashite, hanasa
    3. ite, i, i

III. 1. Iie, [hanasu koto ga] dekimasen.
     2. Iie, [kaeru koto ga] dekimasen.
     3. 20-sai kara [unten ga] dekimasu.
     4. Iie, [oshieru koto ga] dekimasen.
     5. Neru mae ni benkyō-shimasu.
     6. Iie, [hanasu koto ga] dekimasendeshita.
     7. Hai, kesanakereba narimasen.
     8. Iroirona o-miyage o kaimasu.
     9. Hai, [taberu koto ga] dekimasu.
    10. Iie, [utau koto ga] dekimasen.

Dai 19 ka (117 pēji)

I. 1. ni   2. o   3. ni   4. ni
   5. ni   6. ni   7. o   8. ni
   9. ni   10. ni

II. 1. mita, mi, mita
   2. naosu, naoshita, naosa
   3. akaruku, akarukute, akaruku

III. 1. Hai, [mita koto ga] arimasu.
   2. 3-kai [notta koto ga] arimasu.
   3. Hai, [nonda koto ga] arimasu.
   4. Iie, [tabeta koto ga] arimasen.
   5. Kenshū Sentā de Nihon-go o benkyō-shimasu.
   6. Shinkansen de itta hō ga ii desu.
   7. Iie, [kita koto ga] arimasen.
   8. Nihon-go o benkyō-shite, terebi o mimasu.
   9. Nihon-go no benkyō ga owatta ato de, ikimasu.
   10. Hai, arimasu.

Dai 20 ka (123 pēji)

I. itakatta————————————————itakatta desu
    tabenakatta————————————tabemasendeshita
    neta————————————————nemashita
    nonda———————————————nomimashita
    itta—————————————————ikimashita
    300-en datta——————————300-en deshita
    kaetta———————————————kaerimashita
    nonda———————————————nomimashita

I. 1. Hai, [watashi no kazoku wa] genki da to omoimasu.
2. Iie, [kaisha no hito wa ashita] konai to omoimasu.
3. Iie, [ashita shiken ga] nai to omoimasu.
4. Hai, Nihon-go de hanasanakereba naranai to omoimasu.
5. Iie, [Nihon-go wa] muzukashikunai to omoimasu.
6. Hai, [Garcia-san wa] mō byōin e itta to omoimasu.

II. 1. Nihon-go no shiken ga aru
2. kōjō-kengaku wa omoshiroi
3. tomodachi ga kuru
4. Indo-jin
5. kekkon-shite iru
6. Nihon-go ga mada wakaranai
7. niku o zenzen tabenai

III. 1. "Itadakimasu" to iimasu.
2. Kuruma to hito ga ōi kuni da to omoimasu.
3. Hai, genki da to omoimasu.
4. Hai, taihen takai to omoimasu.
5. Iie, furanai to omoimasu.

I. 1. himana 2. kekkon-suru 3. wakaranai
    4. sabishii 5. tsuita 6. konai

II. 1. kusuri o nomimasu
    2. kuraku narimasu
    3. Kekkon-suru
    4. O-sake o nomu
    5. Wakaranai

III. 1. [Samui toki,] ōbā o kimasu.
     2. [Okane ga nai toki,] ginkō kara karimasu.
     3. [Sentā o deru toki, uketsuke no hito ni]
        "Itte mairimasu" to iimasu.
     4. [Byōki no toki,] jimusho e itte kusuri o moraimasu.
     5. [Watashi wa himana toki,] niwa de barēbōru o shimasu.

I. 1. nan   2. doko   3. doko   4. dare
    5. dare   6. dō (nan)   7. doko   8. nani

II. 1. [Watashi ga jisshū-suru kōjō wa] Yokohama ni arimasu.
     2. [Senshū kengaku-shita kōjō wa] Tōkyō-kikai desu.
     3. [Kurasu no naka de kekkon-shite iru hito wa] Tanom-san
         desu.
     4. [Watashi ni Nihon-go o oshiete iru sensei wa]
         Tanaka-san desu.
     5. [Watashi ga issho ni benkyō-shite iru kenshūsei wa]
         Indoneshia to Firipin to Indo no hito desu.
     6. [Watashi ga sukina supōtsu wa] barēbōru desu.
     7. [Watashi ga kiraina tabemono wa] sakana desu.
     8. [Ima made kengaku-shita kōjō no naka de] Tōkyō-kikai ga
         yokatta desu.
     9. [Nihon de watashi ga kaitai mono wa] kamera to rajio desu.
    10. Iie, [watashi wa ima jidōsha o kau okane ga] arimasen.

I. 1. wa   2. wa   3. ga   4. wa
   5. o   6. ga   7. o   8. ga
   9. to, to   10. o

II. 1. [Watashi no shumi wa] barēbōru [o suru koto] to eiga o miru koto desu.
   2. Hai, shitte imashita.
   3. Hai, [watashi wa Ei-go o hanasu koto ga] dekimasu.
   4. Hai, sukoshi [utau koto ga] dekimasu.
   5. Hai, [do-yōbi no gogo benkyō ga nai koto o] shitte imasu.
   6. Asobu koto no hō ga omoshiroi desu.
   7. Bunkai-suru koto no hō ga yasashii desu.
   8. Hai, [Nihon-go o hanasu koto wa] muzukashii to omoimasu.
   9. Iie, amari jōzu dewa arimasen.
   10. Hai, [watashi wa eiga o miru koto ga] taihen suki desu.

Fukushū A (147 pēji) no kotae wa 28 pēji desu.

I.   1. aruite ikimashō
     2. Moshi hima datta
     3. yoroshiku itte kudasai
     4. ureshiku narimasu
     5. wakarimasen

II. 1. Doko   2. dare   3. nani   4. Nan
     5. dō

III. 1. Tōkyō no Ginza e ikimasu.
     2. 9-ji ni kite kudasai.
     3. Heya de yasumimasu.
     4. Tomodachi kara karimasu.
     5. Shinkansen ga ichiban hayai desu.
     6. Jidōsha o kaimasu.
     7. Byōin e itte kudasai.
     8. 3-jikan gurai benkyō-shitara, jōzu ni narimasu
     9. Hai, [ame ga futte mo,] ikimasu.
    10. Hai, [sukoshi atama ga itakute mo,] benkyō-shimasu.

I. 1. Indoneshia-go to Ei-go ga hanasemasu.
   2. Iie, amari yoku neraremasendeshita.
   3. Shatsu ya kutsu ya pen nado ga kaemasu.
   4. Iie, muzukashikute oboeraremasen.
   5. Kōen ga miemasu.
   6. Hai, kikoemasu.
   7. Iie, amari nomemasen.
   8. Hai, shūri-dekimasu.
   9. Iie, mada kakeraremasen.
   10. Iie, naosemasen.

II. 1. I (mō)
   2. II (sugu)
   3. II (zenbu)
   4. I (dandan)
   5. III (yoku)
   6. II (sonnani)

Fukushū B (159 pēji) no kotae wa 28 pēji desu.

I. 1. Indoneshia kara kimashita.
    2. Kaisha e ikimasu.
    3. Koibito ni ichiban aitai desu.
    4. Pan to tamago o tabemasu.
    5. Tanaka-san ga oshiete kudasaimashita.
        (Tanaka-san ni oshiete moraimashita.)
    6. Tokei o katte agemasu.
    7. Rajio o katte moraimashita.
    8. Otōsan ni katte moraimashita.
    9. Kenshū Sentā ni sunde imasu.
    10. Hai, yoku neraremasu (yasumemasu).

II. 1. III (Desukara)
    2. II (Soshite)
    3. I (Sorekara)
    4. II (Keredomo)
    5. III (Dakara)

Fukushū A (147 pēji)

I. 1. de   2. e   3. ni   4. de
    5. e   6. de   7. ni   8. e
    9. ni   10. de

II. 1. ga   2. o   3. o   4. ga
    5. ga   6. o   7. ga   8. ga
    9. o   10. ga

III. 1. ni, o   2. kara, o   3. to, to, ga   4. no
     5. ga   6. mo   7. ga   8. no, ni
     9. ni   10. no, o

Fukushū B (159 pēji)

1. waratte   2. hiite   3. haira
4. kai, iki   5. tabete, shi   6. nuga
7. benkyō-shita   8. okiru   9. notta
10. abite   11. miru   12. hirokute
13. furu, motte itta   14. okuru   15. himana
16. kuraku   17. ko   18. Wakaranakatta
19. yameru   20. Dekakeru, kaketa

Mondai

I.　Rei 1 :　Tōkyō wa (ōkii—ōkii) machi desu.
　　　　　　　Tōkyō wa (ōkii—ōkii) desu.
　　Rei 2 :　Ano hito wa (shinsetsu—shinsetsuna) hito desu.
　　　　　　　Ano hito wa (shinsetsu—shinsetsu) desu.

　　1.　Sakura wa (kirei—　　　) hana desu.
　　　　Sakura wa (kirei—　　　) desu.
　　2.　Sore wa (omoshiroi—　　　) hon desu.
　　　　Sono hon wa (omoshiroi—　　　) desu.
　　3.　Kyōto wa (shizuka—　　　) machi desu.
　　　　Kyōto wa (shizuka—　　　) dewa arimasen.
　　4.　Tōkyō wa (yūmei—　　　) tokoro desu.
　　　　Tōkyō wa (yūmei—　　　) desu.
　　5.　Kore wa (furui—　　　) zasshi desu.
　　　　Kono zasshi wa (furui—　　　) nai desu.

II.　Rei :　Ano depāto wa ōkii desu.
　　　　　—Ano depāto wa ōkikunai desu.
　　1.　Kono kōhii wa tsumetai desu.
　　2.　Sono pen wa warui desu.
　　3.　Watashi no kutsu wa atarashii desu.
　　4.　Kyō wa atsui desu.
　　5.　Kono shiken wa yasashii desu.

III.　1.　Nihon-go wa omoshiroi desu ka.
　　　2.　Anata no kuni wa donna kuni desu ka.
　　　3.　Anata no jisho wa ii desu ka.
　　　4.　Nihon no tabemono wa dō desu ka.
　　　5.　Kenshūsei no heya wa donna heya desu ka.
　　　6.　Anata no sensei wa donna hito desu ka.
　　　7.　Nihon no kudamono wa oishii desu ka.
　　　8.　Sentā wa donna tokoro desu ka.
　　　9.　Fujisan wa takai desu ka, hikui desu ka.
　　　10.　Nihon no tabemono wa yasui desu ka.

Dai 9 Ka

Bunkei

1. Watashi wa ringo ga suki desu.
2. Arora-san wa dansu ga jōzu desu.
3. Watashi wa kanji ga wakarimasen.
4. Watashi wa kodomo ga arimasu.

Kaiwa

Tanaka: Dō shimashita ka.

Rao: Kaze o hikimashita.
Soshite sukoshi atama ga itai desu.

Tanaka: Byōin e ikimashita ka.

Rao: Iie, ikimasen.

Tanaka: Dōshite desu ka.

Rao: Chūsha ga kirai desu kara.

Tanaka: Dewa, kusuri o agemashō ka.

Rao: Ē, onegai-shimasu.

Reibun

1. Anata wa biiru ga suki desu ka.
   —Hai, suki desu.
   —Iie, suki dewa arimasen.

2. Anata wa donna supōtsu ga suki desu ka.
   —Tenisu ga suki desu.

3. Tanom-san wa uta ga jōzu desu ka, heta desu ka.
   —Jōzu desu.

4. Anata wa taipu no tsukai-kata ga wakarimasu ka.
   —Hai, yoku wakarimasu.
   —Iie, zenzen wakarimasen.

5. Anata wa okane ga ikura arimasu ka.
   —100-en dake arimasu.

6. Watashi wa onaka ga itai desu kara, heya de nemasu.

7. Dōshite kaisha o yasumimashita ka.
   —Sukoshi netsu ga arimashita kara.

Renshū A

1. Watashi wa | ringo | ga suki desu.
    | sakana |
    | niku |
    | eiga |
    | tabako |

    Anata wa | nani | .... ka.

2. Anata wa | donna | kudamono | ga suki desu ka.
    | ongaku |
    | supōtsu |
    | ryōri |

3. Arora-san wa | dansu | ga taihen jōzu desu.
    | uta |
    | ryōri |
    | tenisu |
    | Nihon-go |

4. Watashi wa | kanji | ga yoku wakarimasu.
    | hiragana |
    | Tai-go |
    | Ei-go |
    | taipu no tsukai-kata |

5. Watashi wa | kodomo | ga takusan arimasu.
    | tomodachi |
    | okane |
    | rekōdo |

Renshū B

1. 1) Rei: Watashi wa <u>niku</u> ga kirai desu.
      (sakana, biiru, ano hito, kusuri, benkyō, butaniku)
   2) Rei: Watashi wa <u>Nihon-go</u> ga heta desu.
      (uta, dansu, pinpon, ryōri, Ei-go, taipu)

2. Rei: Anata wa donna <u>supōtsu</u> ga suki desu ka. (pinpon)
        —<u>Pinpon</u> ga suki desu.
   1) (kudamono   :   banana)
   2) (tabemono   :   Chūgoku-ryōri)
   3) (uta   :   Nihon no uta)
   4) (nomimono   :   o-sake)

3. Rei: Rao-san wa <u>Nihon-go</u> ga jōzu desu ka, heta desu ka.
       (uta, dansu, pinpon, gitā, ryōri)

4. Rei 1: Anata wa toriniku ga suki desu ka. (hai, taihen)
          —Hai, taihen suki desu.
   Rei 2: Anata wa butaniku ga suki desu ka. (iie, amari)
          —Iie, amari suki dewa arimasen.
   Rei 3: Anata wa yasai ga suki desu ka. (iie)
          —Iie, [suki dewa arimasen,] kirai desu.
   1) Kimura-san wa dansu ga jōzu desu ka. (hai, taihen) —
   2) Anata wa taipu ga jōzu desu ka. (iie) —
   3) Anata wa gyūnyū ga suki desu ka. (iie, amari) —
   4) Slamet-san wa uta ga heta desu ka. (iie) —
   5) Anata wa Nihon no tabemono ga suki desu ka. (iie, amari) —
   6) Anata wa supōtsu ga kirai desu ka. (iie) —

5. Rei: Watashi wa okane ga <u>takusan</u> arimasu.
      (sukoshi, zenzen, 50-en, amari)

6. Rei: Anata wa Nihon-go ga wakarimasu ka. (yoku)
    —Hai, yoku wakarimasu.
    1) (kanji   :   sukoshi)
    2) (hiragana   :   amari)
    3) (taipu no tsukai-kata   :   yoku)
    4) (Ei-go   :   mochiron)
    5) (hashi no tsukai-kata   :   zenzen)

7. Rei: Okane ga 100-en arimasu.
    —Okane ga 100-en dake arimasu.
    1) Okane ga sukoshi arimasu. —
    2) Nihon-go o sukoshi benkyō-shimasu. —
    3) Nihon-go o 1-jikan benkyō-shimasu. —
    4) Kanji ga sukoshi wakarimasu. —
    5) Kyō kaisha o yasumimasu. —

8. Rei: atama ga itai desu, kaisha o yasumimasu
    —Atama ga itai desu kara, kaisha o yasumimasu.
    1) onaka ga itai desu, nani mo tabemasen —
    2) netsu ga arimasu, heya de yasumimasu —
    3) samui desu, kaze o hikimashita —
    4) jidōsha ga arimasen, aruite ikimasu —
    5) benkyō-shimashita, yoku wakarimasu —
    6) imi ga wakarimasen, jisho o mimasu —

9. Rei: Dōshite gohan o tabemasen ka. (onaka ga itai desu)
    —Onaka ga itai desu kara.
    1) (issho ni ikimasen   :   sukoshi netsu ga arimasu)
    2) (Tōkyō e ikimasen   :   okane ga arimasen)
    3) (atama ga itai desu   :   kinō no ban o-sake o nomimashita)
    4) (terebi ga kirai desu   :   omoshirokunai desu)
    5) (o-sake o nomimasen   :   o-sake ga kirai desu)

Mondai

I. Rei: Watashi wa sakana ga suki desu.
   —Watashi wa sakana ga suki dewa arimasen.
1. Arora-san wa tenisu ga jōzu desu
2. Watashi wa kanji ga wakarimasu.
3. Watashi wa tabako ga suki desu.
4. Watashi wa kodomo ga arimasu.
5. Kono bōrupen wa watashi no desu.

II. Rei: Taihen atsui desu kara, (mizu o nomimasu).
1. Kinō no ban biiru o nomimashita kara, (   ).
2. (   ) kara, Nihon-go ga wakarimasen.
3. Chūsha ga kirai desu kara, (   ).
4. (   ) kara, doko e mo ikimasen.
5. Byōki desu kara, (   ).

III. 1. Anata wa yasai ga suki desu ka.
2. Anata wa donna nomimono ga suki desu ka.
3. Anata wa o-sake ga suki desu ka, kirai desu ka.
4. Anata wa pinpon ga jōzu desu ka.
5. Anata wa taipu no tsukai-kata ga wakarimasu ka.
6. Anata wa Ei-go ga wakarimasu ka.
7. Anata wa okane ga ikura arimasu ka.
8. Anata wa katakana ga wakarimasu ka.
9. Anata wa okusan ga arimasu ka.
10. Anata wa donna supōtsu ga suki desu ka.

Dai 10 Ka

Bunkei

1. Kyōshitsu ni kenshūsei ga imasu.
2. Tsukue no ue ni hon ga arimasu.
3. Tanaka-san wa jimusho ni imasu.
4. Ginkō wa yūbinkyoku no tonari ni arimasu.
5. Sentā no chikaku ni depāto ya resutoran ya byōin [nado] ga arimasu.

Kaiwa

Ali: Tanaka-san wa jimusho ni imasu ka.

Kimura: Mō uchi e kaerimashita.

Ali: Tanaka-san no uchi wa doko desu ka.

Kimura: Eki no mae ni hana-ya ga arimasu ne.

               Tanaka-san no uchi wa hana-ya no tonari desu.

Ali: Sō desu ka.

               Dewa, korekara ikimasu.

Kimura: Itte irasshai.

Ali: Itte mairimasu.

Reibun

1. Asoko ni dare ga imasu ka.
   —Kenshūsei ga imasu.
   —Dare mo imasen.

2. Hako no naka ni nani ga arimasu ka.
   —Boruto to natto ga arimasu.
   —Nani mo arimasen.

3. Tanaka-san wa doko ni imasu ka.
   —Robii ni imasu.

4. Depāto wa doko ni arimasu ka.
   —Eki no chikaku ni arimasu.

5. Suitchi wa doko desu ka.
   —Doa no migi desu.

6. Nagoya wa Tōkyō to Ōsaka no aida ni arimasu.

7. Jimusho wa 2-kai no robii no hidari desu.

Renshū A

1. Kyōshitsu ni | kenshūsei | ga imasu.
   Rao-san
   hito
   onna no hito
   dare .... ka.

2. Asoko ni | kagi | ga arimasu.
   tokei
   kōen
   gakkō
   nani .... ka.

3. Hako no | ue | ni hon ga arimasu.
   shita
   naka
   migi
   hidari

4. Tanaka-san wa | jimusho | ni imasu.
   soto
   Lee-san no ushiro
   doko .... ka.

5. Ginkō wa | asoko | ni arimasu.
   chikaku
   depāto no tonari
   doko .... ka.

6. Sentā no chikaku ni | depāto | ya | resutoran | ya | byōin | [nado] ga
   ginkō | yūbinkyoku | toko-ya
   gakkō | kōen | kōjō
   arimasu.

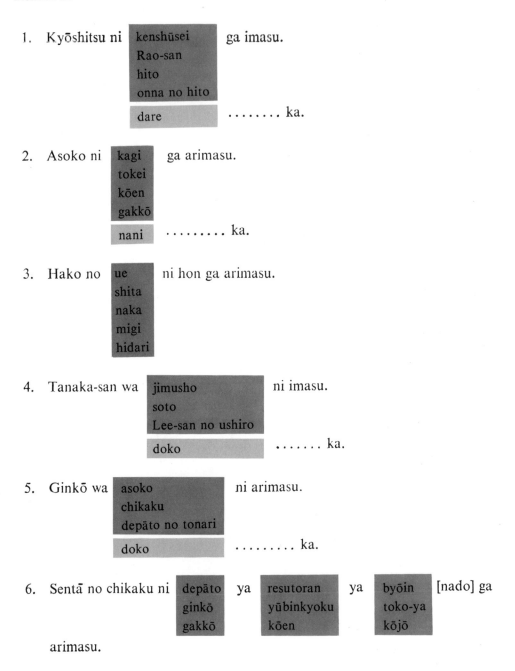

— 60 —

Renshū B

1. Rei: <u>Kenshūsei</u> ga imasu.

    /hako, tsukue, sensei, okane, kodomo, resutoran,\
    (tabako to matchi, tomodachi, Rao-san, watashi no kagi,)
    \ *dare mo, *nani mo /

2. Rei: <u>Kyōshitsu</u> ni kenshūsei ga imasu.

    (robii, niwa, shokudō, asoko, watashi no kaisha)

3. Rei: <u>Tsukue</u> no ue ni hon ga arimasu.

    (terebi, shinbun, hako, isu, zasshi)

4. Chāto 6

    Rei: <u>Tsukue no ue</u> ni nani ga arimasu ka. (hon)
    —<u>Hon</u> ga arimasu.

1)	(tsukue no shita	:	kaban)
2)	(Kimura-san no migi	:	isu)
3)	(uchi no soto	:	isu)
4)	(byōin no tonari	:	hana-ya)
5)	(eki no mae	:	depāto)
6)	(kaisha no hidari	:	ginkō)
7)	(gakkō no chikaku	:	ginkō ya hana-ya)
8)	(uchi no naka	:	tsukue ya isu)

5. Rei: <u>Kagi</u> wa hako no <u>shita</u> ni arimasu.

    (ue, naka, soto, mae, tonari, ushiro, migi, hidari)

6. Rei: <u>Kagi</u> wa doko ni arimasu ka.

    (pen, kami, haizara, nōto, hako, jisho, isu, tsukue)

7. Chāto 6

Rei: Hon wa doko ni arimasu ka. (tsukue no ue)
—Tsukue no ue ni arimasu.

1) (kōen : gakkō no mae)
2) (kaisha : yūbinkyoku no hidari)
3) (Kimura-san : uchi no naka)
4) (jidōsha : depāto no ushiro)
5) (kaban : tsukue no shita)
6) (Ali-san : niwa)
7) (posuto : yūbinkyoku no mae)
8) (byōin : hana-ya no tonari)

8. Chāto 6

Rei: Hon wa doko ni arimasu ka. — Tsukue no ue ni arimasu.
1) Tsukue no ue ni shinbun ga arimasu ka. —
2) Isu wa doko ni arimasu ka. —
3) Gakkō no niwa ni dare ga imasu ka. —
4) Kimura-san wa doko desu ka. —
5) Eki no mae ni nani ga arimasu ka. —
6) Yūbinkyoku to ginkō no aida ni nani ga arimasu ka. —
7) Slamet-san wa doko ni imasu ka. —
8) Resutoran wa doko desu ka. —

9. Rei: Sentā ni doko no kuni no hito ga imasu ka.
—Indo-jin ya Firipin-jin nado ga imasu.

Burajiru-jin : Chūgoku-jin, Echiopia-jin : Firipin-jin,
Indo-jin : Indoneshia-jin, Iran-jin : Kankoku-jin,
Mekishiko-jin : Ōsutoraria-jin, Perū-jin : Tai-jin

Mondai

I. Rei: Hon ga (arimasu).

2-kai ni otoko no hito ga (imasu).

1. Chikaku ni biru ga ( ).
2. Heya ni dare mo ( ).
3. Ginkō wa eki no mae ni ( ).
4. Sentā ni iroiro no kuni no hito ga ( ).
5. Tai no Tanom-san wa jimusho ni ( ).

II. Rei: (○) Tsukue no ue ni shinbun ga arimasu.

(×) Denwa wa tsukue no ue ni arimasu.

1. (　) Tsukue no shita ni kagi ga arimasu.
2. (　) Arora-san wa doa no mae ni imasu.
3. (　) Heya ni Lee-san ga imasu.
4. (　) Rajio no ue ni haizara to matchi ga arimasu.
5. (　) Terebi no ushiro ni nani mo arimasen.

III. 1. Anata wa ima doko ni imasu ka.
2. Anata no tsukue no ue ni nani ga arimasu ka.
3. Denki no suitchi wa doko ni arimasu ka.
4. Anata no kuni no taishikan wa doko ni arimasu ka.
5. Sentā ni kenshūsei ga takusan imasu ka.
6. Anata no pasupōto wa doko ni arimasu ka.
7. Kyōshitsu ni doko no kuni no hito ga imasu ka.
8. Anata no heya ni ima dare ga imasu ka.
9. Anata no otōsan wa ima doko ni imasu ka.
10. Sentā no chikaku ni depāto ga arimasu ka.

Dai 11 Ka

Bunkei

1. Ringo ga hitotsu arimasu.
2. Kenshūsei ga futari imasu.
3. Rao-san wa Nihon de 6-kagetsu jisshū-shimasu.
4. Watashi wa 1-shūkan ni 1-kai sentaku-shimasu.

Kaiwa

Cortez:	Kono kōjō ni hito ga nan-nin imasu ka.
Kōjō no hito:	400-nin gurai desu.
Cortez:	Kikai ga nan-dai arimasu ka.
Kōjō no hito:	30-dai arimasu.
Cortez:	Gaikoku-sei desu ka.
Kōjō no hito:	Iie, zenbu Nihon-sei desu.
Cortez:	1-nichi ni donokurai kamera o tsukurimasu ka.
Kōjō no hito:	100-dai desu.

Reibun

1. Sentā ni kyōshitsu ga ikutsu arimasu ka.
   —Mittsu arimasu.

2. Anata no kaisha ni kenshūsei ga nan-nin imasu ka.
   —6-nin imasu.

3. Anata wa kodomo ga nan-nin arimasu ka.
   —Futari arimasu.

4. Kenshūsei wa Nihon de nan-kagetsu jisshū-shimasu ka.
   —6-kagetsu gurai jisshū-shimasu.

5. Anata wa donokurai Nihon ni imasu ka.
   —1-nen imasu.

6. Anata wa 1-shūkan ni nan-kai tegami o kakimasu ka.
   —2-kai kakimasu.

7. Kono ringo wa hitotsu ikura desu ka.
   —Hitotsu 50-en desu.
   Dewa, mittsu kudasai.
   —Zenbu de 150-en desu.

8. 15-en no kitte o 3-mai kudasai.

9. Kono kōjō de jidōsha o 1-nichi ni 1,400-dai tsukurimasu.

Renshū A

1. Ringo ga | hitotsu | arimasu.
   | futatsu |
   | mittsu |
   | yottu |
   | itsutsu |
   | ikutsu | .... ka.

2. Kenshūsei ga | hitori | imasu.
   | futari |
   | san-nin |
   | yo-nin |
   | nan-nin | ..... ka.

3. Rao-san wa Nihon de | 6-kagetsu | jisshū-shimasu.
   | 2-nen |
   | 12-shūkan |

   Anata wa Nihon de | donokurai | .... ka.

4. Watashi wa | 1-nichi | ni 1-kai sōji-shimasu.
   | 1-shūkan |
   | 1-kagetsu |

5. 15-en no kitte o | 1-mai | kudasai.
   | 2-mai |
   | 3-mai |

6. Watashi wa rajio o | 1-dai | kaimashita.
   | 2-dai |
   | 3-dai |

7. Kore wa | hitotsu | 100-en desu.
   | 1-mai |

Renshū B

1. Rei: Ringo ga ikutsu arimasu ka. (1)
   —Hitotsu arimasu.

1)	(haizara	:	2)		6)	(kagi	:	5)
2)	(tamago	:	4)		7)	(kaban	:	7)
3)	(tsukue	:	6)		8)	(kōjō	:	9)
4)	(heya	:	3)		9)	(kuni	:	11)
5)	(isu	:	8)		10)	(tokei	:	10)

2. Rei: Anata wa kazoku ga nan-nin arimasu ka. (6)
   —Roku-nin arimasu.

1)	(kodomo	:	3)
2)	(kyōdai	:	2)
3)	(tomodachi	:	4)
4)	(onna no kyōdai	:	*zenzen)
5)	(Nihon-jin no tomodachi	:	1)

3. Rei: Watashi wa Nihon ni imasu. (3-nen)
   —Watashi wa Nihon ni 3-nen imasu.
   1) Watashi wa mainichi nemasu. (8-jikan) —
   2) Sentā de Nihon-go o benkyō-shimasu. (5-shūkan) —
   3) Watashi wa heya de yasumimasu. (30-pun) —
   4) Ōsaka no kōjō de jisshū-shimasu. (2-kagetsu) —
   5) Watashi wa kaisha o yasumimashita. (1-nen) —

4. Rei: Maiban nan-jikan nemasu ka. (7)
   —Nana-jikan nemasu.
   1) Sentā ni nan-nichi imasu ka. (15) —
   2) Sentā de nan-shūkan benkyō-shimasu ka. (5) —
   3) Nihon de nan-kagetsu jisshū-shimasu ka. (8) —
   4) Gakkō e nan-nen ikimashita ka. (16) —
   5) Sentā kara eki made nan-pun kakarimasu ka. (30) —

5. Rei: tegami o kakimasu (1-shūkan, 2-kai)
    —1-shūkan ni 2-kai tegami o kakimasu.

    1) denwa o kakemasu (1-nichi, 1-kai) —
    2) sentaku-shimasu (1-shūkan, 1-kai) —
    3) kusuri o nomimasu (1-nichi, 3-kai) —
    4) eiga o mimasu (1-kagetsu, 2-kai) —
    5) Kyōto e ikimasu (1-nen, 1-kai) —

6. Rei: Kikai ga 2-dai arimasu.
    (jidōsha, Nihon-jin, kami, kyōshitsu, sensei,
    ringo, shatsu, terebi   )

7. Rei: Shatsu o nan-mai kaimashita ka.
    (kippu, ringo, kamera, kitte, hako, rajio)

8. Rei: Watashi wa shatsu o kaimashita. (2)
    —Watashi wa shatsu o 2-mai kaimashita.

    1) Tomodachi ni rekōdo o agemashita. (2) —
    2) Asoko ni jidōsha ga arimasu. (5) —
    3) Watashi-tachi wa ringo o tabemashita. (8) —
    4) 60-en no kitte o kudasai. (3) —
    5) Nihon de kamera o kaimashita. (2) —
    6) Sentā ni kyōshitsu ga arimasu. (4) —

9. Rei: 9-ji kara 12-ji made benkyō-shimasu
    —3-jikan benkyō-shimasu.

    1) 5-ji kara 7-ji made hatarakimashita —
    2) 9-ji kara 12-ji han made Nihon-go desu —
    3) 10-ji kara 10-ji 10-pun made yasumimasu —
    4) getsu-yōbi kara kin-yōbi made Nihon-go o naraimasu —
    5) 1-gatsu 15-nichi kara 6-gatsu 30-nichi made Niohn ni imasu —

Mondai

I. Rei: ringo ga arimasu (3) — Ringo ga mittsu arimasu.
1. kenshūsei ga imasu (1) —
2. jidōsha ga arimasu (5) —
3. ringo o tabemashita (2) —
4. kikai ga arimasu (50) —
5. kami o moraimashita (3) —

II. Rei: Jimusho ni taipu ga 2-dai arimasu. Robii ni 1-dai arimasu.
Zenbu de nan-dai arimasu ka. — 3-dai arimasu.
1. Kimura-san wa Ginza de rekōdo o 3-mai kaimashita. 1-mai Rao-san ni agemashita. Ima Kimura-san wa rekōdo ga nan-mai arimasu ka. —
2. Ali-san wa okusan to kodomo ga futari arimasu. Ali-san no kazoku wa zenbu de nan-nin desu ka. —
3. Lee-san kara tamago o muttsu moraimashita. Kesa futatsu tabemashita. Ima tamago ga ikutsu arimasu ka. —
4. Kitte o 5-mai kaimasu. 1-mai 60-en desu. Zenbu de ikura desu ka. —
5. Nihon ni 6-kagetsu imasu. Sentā de 1-kagetsu han benkyō-shimashita. Korekara nan-kagetsu imasu ka. —

III. 1. Anata wa maiban nan-jikan benkyō-shimasu ka.
2. Anata wa 1-shūkan ni nan-kai tegami o kakimasu ka.
3. Kenshūsei wa Sentā de donokurai Nihon-go o naraimasu ka.
4. Anata wa kōjō de nan-kagetsu jisshū-shimasu ka.
5. Anata wa kyōdai ga nan-nin arimasu ka.
6. Sentā kara eki made aruite donokurai desu ka.
7. Sentā ni kyōshitsu ga ikutsu arimasu ka.
8. Sentā ni ima kenshūsei ga nan-nin imasu ka.
9. 1-kagetsu wa nan-shūkan desu ka.
10. 1-shūkan wa nan-nichi desu ka.

Dai 12 Ka

Bunkei

1. Tōkyō wa Ōsaka yori ōkii desu.
2. Kudamono no naka de banana ga ichiban suki desu.
3. Kinō wa ame deshita.
4. Ototoi wa samukatta desu.

Kaiwa

Kimura : Ii o-tenki desu ne.
　　　　O-shigoto wa dō desu ka.
Ali : 　Ē, itsumo isogashii desu.
　　　　Tokidoki, yoru mo hatarakimasu.
Kimura : Anata wa itsu ga ichiban hima desu ka.
Ali : 　Sō desu ne.
　　　　Do-yōbi no yoru ga ichiban hima desu.
Kimura : Watashi no uchi e kimasen ka.
Ali : 　Ē, nan-ji goro ga ii desu ka.
Kimura : 5-ji goro ga ii desu.

Reibun

1. Ei-go to Nihon-go to, dochira ga muzukashii desu ka.
   —Ei-go no hō ga muzukashii desu.
   —Ryōhō muzukashii desu.

2. Tai to Indo to Iran to, doko ga ichiban chikai desu ka.
   —Tai ga ichiban chikai desu.

3. Tanom-san to Lee-san to Rao-san to, dare ga ichiban wakai desu ka.
   —Rao-san ga ichiban wakai desu.

4. Fune to hikōki to densha to, dore ga ichiban hayai desu ka.
   —Hikōki ga ichiban hayai desu.

5. Supōtsu no naka de nani ga ichiban suki desu ka.
   —Pinpon ga ichiban suki desu.

6. Kinō wa yasumi deshita ka.
   —Hai, yasumi deshita.
   —Iie, yasumi dewa arimasendeshita.

7. Ryokō wa tanoshikatta desu ka.
   —Hai, tanoshikatta desu.
   Tenki wa dō deshita ka.
   —Amari yokunakatta desu.

Renshū A

1. Tōkyō wa | Ōsaka | yori ōkii desu.
   - Yokohama
   - Nagoya
   - Kyōto
   - Hiroshima

2. Densha to basu to, | dochira | ga | hayai | desu ka.
   - yasui
   - omoshiroi
   - suki

   —Densha [no hō] ga | hayai | desu.
   - yasui
   - omoshiroi
   - suki

3. Tanom-san to Lee-san to Rao-san to, | dare | ga ichiban | toshi-ue | desu ka.
   - wakai
   - isogashii
   - genki

   —Lee-san ga ichiban | toshi-ue | desu.
   - wakai
   - isogashii
   - genki

4. | ame | deshita ⟶ | ame | dewa arimasendeshita
   - ii tenki
   - yasumi
   - hima

5. | samu | katta | desu ⟶ | samu | kunakatta | desu
   - isogashi katta ⟶ isogashi kunakatta
   - tanoshi katta ⟶ tanoshi kunakatta

— 72 —

Renshū B

1. Rei: <u>Shinkansen</u> wa <u>basu</u> yori <u>hayai</u> desu.
   1) (fune, hikōki, osoi)
   2) (Kyōto, Ōsaka, shizuka)
   3) (Rao-san, Lee-san, toshi-ue)
   4) (Echiopia, Chūgoku, tōi)
   5) (Arora-san, Tanaka-san, wakai)
   6) (Kankoku, Mekishiko, chikai)
   7) (Indo, Nihon, hito ga ōi)
   8) (Tai, Nihon, jidōsha ga sukunai)

2. Rei: <u>Hikōki</u> to <u>jidōsha</u> to dochira ga hayai desu ka.
   1) (fune, hikōki)
   2) (takushii, basu)
   3) (shinkansen, jidōsha)
   4) (basu, chikatetsu)
   5) (hikōki, shinkansen)

3. Rei: <u>Burajiru</u> to <u>Nihon</u> to dochira ga <u>ōkii</u> desu ka. (Burajiru)
        —<u>Burajiru</u> no hō ga ōkii desu.
   1) (hikōki, jidōsha, hayai   :   hikōki)
   2) (pinpon, tenisu, omoshiroi   :   tenisu)
   3) (terebi, rajio, yasui   :   rajio)
   4) (Ei-go, Nihon-go, yasashii   :   *ryōhō)
   5) (supōtsu, ongaku, suki   :   supōtsu)
   6) (kyō, ashita, isogashii   :   ashita)
   7) (8-gatsu, 9-gatsu, suzushii   :   9-gatsu)
   8) (Ali-san, Slamet-san, toshi-ue   :   Ali-san)

4. Rei: Yokohama to Kyōto to Nagoya to, doko ga ichiban <u>ōkii</u> desu ka.
   (kirei, furui, yūmei, omoshiroi, atsui, hito ga ōi)

5. Rei: <u>Ringo</u> to <u>banana</u> to <u>mikan</u> to, dore ga ichiban suki desu ka.
(kōhii, kōcha, gyūnyū) (biiru, jūsu, o-sake)
(pinpon, tenisu, futtobōru) (ongaku, supōtsu, benkyō)
(niku, yasai, sakana)

6. Rei: Tōkyō to Yokohama to Ōsaka to, doko ga ichiban ōkii desu ka.
(Tōkyō) — Tōkyō ga ichiban ōkii desu.

1) Tanom-san to Abebe-san to Cortez-san to, dare ga ichiban toshi-ue desu
   ka. (Abebe-san) —
2) Sentā no naka de, dare ga ichiban kirei desu ka. (Kimura-san) —
3) Kōhii to kōcha to jūsu to, dore ga ichiban suki desu ka. (kōcha) —
4) Shinkansen to basu to takushii to, dore ga ichiban hayai desu ka. (shinkansen) —
5) Nichi-yōbi to do-yōbi to getsu-yōbi to, itsu ga ichiban hima desu ka.
   (do-yōbi) —
6) Kurasu no naka de dare ga ichiban hansamu desu ka. (Tanom-san) —
7) Supōtsu no naka de nani ga ichiban suki desu ka. (tenisu) —

7. Rei 1: ame desu — ame deshita
   Rei 2: atsui desu — atsukatta desu

   1) kumori desu —   6) omoshiroi desu —
   2) suki desu —   7) isogashii desu —
   3) hima desu —   8) tanoshii desu —
   4) genki desu —   9) ii desu —
   5) ii tenki desu —   10) hayai desu —

8. Rei: Tanaka-san wa genki deshita ka.
          —Iie, genki dewa arimasendeshita.
   1) Kyōto wa shizuka deshita ka. —
   2) Kinō wa samukatta desu ka. —
   3) Shiken wa muzukashikatta desu ka. —
   4) Ano hito wa Nihon-go ga jōzu deshita ka. —
   5) Kinō wa ame deshita ka. —
   6) Kinō wa isogashikatta desu ka. —

Mondai

I. Rei: ōkii — chiisai

1. ii —
2. samui —
3. muzukashii —
4. isogashii —
5. jōzu —

6. yasui —
7. kirai —
8. toshi-ue —
9. chikai —
10. osoi —

II.
1. Rao-san to Lee-san to, (   ) ga wakai desu ka.
2. Sekai de ichiban takai yama wa (   ) desu ka.
3. Toriniku to butaniku to gyūniku to, (   ) ga ichiban suki desu ka.
4. Indoneshia to Mekishiko to Nihon to, (   ) ga ichiban atsui desu ka.
5. Nihon-ryōri no naka de (   ) ga ichiban oishii desu ka.
6. Kenshūsei no naka de (   ) ga ichiban toshi-ue desu ka.

III.
1. Kōhii to kōcha to, dochira ga suki desu ka.
2. Gyūniku to butaniku to, toriniku to dore ga ichiban suki desu ka.
3. Kurasu no naka de dare ga ichiban toshi-ue desu ka.
4. Do-yōbi to nichi-yōbi to, dochira ga hima desu ka.
5. Benkyō to shigoto to ryokō to, dore ga ichiban omoshiroi desu ka.
6. Nihon de 1-gatsu to 5-gatsu to, 9-gatsu to itsu ga ichiban samui desu ka.
7. Kinō wa ame deshita ka.
8. Kyō no shiken wa muzukashikatta desu ka.
9. Nihon wa Indo yori atsui desu ka.
10. Anata no kuni de ichiban yūmeina tabemono wa nan desu ka.

Dai 13 Ka

Bunkei

1. Watashi wa kamera ga hoshii desu.
2. Watashi wa eiga o (ga) mitai desu.
3. Watashi wa shokudō e gohan o tabe ni ikimasu.
4. Watashi wa Nihon e denki no benkyō ni kimashita.

Kaiwa

Rao: Doko e ikimasu ka.
Lee: Depāto e rajio o kai ni ikimasu.
Rao: Watashi mo rajio ga hoshii desu.
Lee: Dewa, issho ni ikimashō.

Lee: Tsukaremashita ne.
Rao: Watashi wa nodo ga kawakimashita.
　　　Biiru ga nomitai desu ne.
Lee: Ano resutoran ni hairimashō ka.
Rao: Ē, sō shimashō.

Reibun

1. Anata wa nani ga hoshii desu ka.
   —Jidōsha ga hoshii desu.
   —Nani mo hoshikunai desu.

2. Anata wa donna kamera ga hoshii desu ka.
   —Chiisai kamera ga hoshii desu.

3. Anata wa nani o yomitai desu ka.
   —Tai no shinbun o yomitai desu.
   —Nani mo yomitakunai desu.

4. Anata wa nani o shitai desu ka.
   —Kyōto o kenbutsu-shitai desu.

5. Anata wa nani o nomitai desu ka.
   —Nan demo ii desu.

6. Anata wa doko e o-miyage o kai ni ikimasu ka.
   —Depāto e kai ni ikimasu.

7. Anata wa Tōkyō e nani o shi ni ikimasu ka.
   —Tomodachi ni ai ni ikimasu.

8. Nihon e nan no benkyō ni kimashita ka.
   —Erebētā no benkyō ni kimashita.

9. Doko e asobi ni ikitai desu ka.
   —Shinjuku e ikitai desu.

Renshū A

1.

nomi	tai desu		nomi	takunai desu
nomi	masu		nomi	masen
kaeri	masu		kaeri	masen
ai	masu		ai	masen
hataraki	masu		hataraki	masen
kekkon-shi	masu		kekkon-shi	masen
de	masu		de	masen
kaki	masu		kaki	masen
ki	masu		ki	masen
age	masu		age	masen
kenbutsu-shi	masu		kenbutsu-shi	masen
yasumi	masu		yasumi	masen

2.

1) Watashi wa 　kamera　 ga hoshii desu.
　　　　　　　koibito
　　　　　　　jidōsha
　　　　　　　okane
　　　　　　　ii jisho

　　Anata wa 　nani　 ………… ka.

2) Watashi wa 　eiga o mi　tai　 desu.
　　　　　　　ringo o tabe　tai
　　　　　　　Tōkyō e iki　tai
　　　　Kimura-san ni ai　tai

3) Watashi wa shokudō e 　gohan o tabe　 ni ikimasu.
　　　　　　　　　　　　mizu o nomi
　　　　　　　　　　　　terebi o mi
　　　　　　　　　　　　rekōdo o kiki

　　Anata wa ………… 　nani o shi　 …… ka.

4) 　Nan　 demo ii desu.
　　Doko
　　Dare
　　Itsu
　　Dochira

Renshū B

1. Rei: Anata wa donna <u>uchi</u> ga hoshii desu ka. (ōkii uchi)
   —<u>Ōkii uchi</u> ga hoshii desu.
   1) (kamera   :   karui kamera)
   2) (nomimono   :   atsui kōhii)
   3) (terebi   :   karā-terebi)
   4) (rajio   :   toranjisutā-rajio)
   5) (tēpu-rekōdā   :   kasetto)

2. Chāto 5
   1) Rei: (gohan o tabemasu) — gohan o tabetai desu
                                  6) (rekōdo o kikimasu)
   2) (hana o kaimasu)   7) (hon o yomimasu)
   3) (tabako o suimasu)   8) (tegami o kakimasu)
   4) (kōhii o nomimasu)   9) (terebi o mimasu)
   5) (shashin o torimasu)   10) (Nihon-go o benkyō-shimasu)

3. Rei: Nani o nomitai desu ka. (biiru)
        —Biiru o nomitai desu.
   1) Doko e ikitai desu ka. (Ginza) —
   2) Doko o kenbutsu-shitai desu ka. (Kyōto) —
   3) Dare ni aitai desu ka. (Arora-san) —
   4) Nan no kōjō o kengaku-shitai desu ka. (denki no kōjō) —
   5) Nani o shitai desu ka. (nani mo) —
   6) Doko e ikitai desu ka. (doko mo) —
   7) Nani ga hoshii desu ka. (nani mo) —

4. 1) Rei: Depāto e <u>kamera</u> o kai ni ikimashita.
           (nekutai, tokei, hon, shatsu, kutsu, kusuri, rekōdo)
   2) Rei: Watashi wa <u>sanpo</u> ni ikimasu.
           (kaimono, kenbutsu, kengaku, jisshū, sentaku)
   3) Rei: Watashi wa Nihon e <u>denki</u> no benkyō ni kimashita.
           (jidōsha, erebētā, terebi, tēpu-rekōdā)

5. Chāto 5

   1) Rei: (shokudō) — shokudō e gohan o tabe ni ikimasu

                                     6) (tomodachi no heya)

   2) (depāto)   7) (robii)

   3) (robii)   8) (watashi no heya)

   4) (resutoran)   9) (robii)

   5) (niwa)   10) (kyōshitsu)

6. Rei: Doko e o-miyage o kai ni ikimasu ka. (depāto)

       —Depāto e kai ni ikimasu.

   1) (denwa o kakemasu   :   uketsuke)

   2) (kaimono-shimasu   :   Ginza)

   3) (asobimasu   :   tomodachi no uchi)

   4) (jisshū-shimasu   :   Nagoya no kōjō)

   5) (tegami o dashimasu   :   yūbinkyoku)

7. Rei: Shokudō e nani o shi ni ikimashita ka.

       (gohan o tabemasu) — Gohan o tabe ni ikimashita.

   1) (uketsuke   :   kitte o kaimasu)

   2) (Tōkyō   :   Tanom-san ni aimasu)

   3) (Kyōto   :   kenbutsu-shimasu)

   4) (ginkō   :   okane o kaemasu)

   5) (ano kaisha   :   katarogu o moraimasu)

8. Rei 1: Ano resutoran ni hairimashō ka. (ē)

         —Ē, hairimashō.

   Rei 2: Doko e ikimashō ka. (doko demo)

         —Doko demo ii desu.

   1) Gohan o tabemashō ka. (ē) —

   2) Nani o tabemashō ka. (Chūgoku-ryōri) —

   3) Nani o mimashō ka. (nan demo) —

   4) Issho ni benkyō-shimashō ka. (ē) —

   5) Nan-ji ni aimashō ka. (nan-ji demo) —

Mondai

I. Rei: <u>Ringo o</u> tabetai desu. — Nani o tabetai desu ka.
   1. <u>Tōkyō e</u> ikitai desu.
   2. <u>Ashita</u> ano hito ni aitai desu.
   3. Nihon de <u>denki o benkyō-shitai</u> desu.
   4. <u>Arora-san to</u> kekkon-shitai desu.
   5. <u>Uketsuke e</u> kitte o kai ni ikimasu.
   6. <u>Ōkii</u> jidōsha ga hoshii desu.
   7. Depāto e <u>kamera o</u> kai ni ikimasu.
   8. <u>Nani mo</u> hoshikunai desu.

II.   Watashi wa Firipin ☐ Garcia desu. Rao-san ☐ watashi no ichiban ii tomodachi desu. Rao-san wa Indo ☐ kimashita. Watashi-tachi wa mainichi Nihon-go ☐ benkyō-shimasu. Iroirona kuni ☐ kenshūsei ☐ issho desu. Kenshūsei no naka de watashi ☐ ichi-ban wakai desu. Nihon-go ☐ muzukashii desu ga, omoshiroi desu. Demo watashi wa shiken ☐ amari suki dewa arimasen. Raishū Sentā ☐ demasu. Soshite Ōsaka ☐ kōjō ☐ jisshū ni ikimasu. Kōjō de 4-kagetsu kikai ☐ jisshū-shimasu. Rao-san no kōjō wa Yokohama ☐ arimasu.

III. 1. Anata wa Nihon e nani o shi ni kimashita ka.
   2. Anata wa donna kamera ga hoshii desu ka.
   3. Ima dare ni ichiban aitai desu ka.
   4. Anata wa okane to hima to, dochira ga hoshii desu ka.
   5. Nan no kōjō o kengaku-shitai desu ka.
   6. Nichi-yōbi ni doko e ikitai desu ka.
   7. Ginkō e nani o shi ni ikimasu ka.
   8. Nihon de donna ryōri ga tabetai desu ka.
   9. Doko e asobi ni ikitai desu ka.
   10. Anata wa itsu kōjō-kengaku ni ikimashita ka.

Dai 14 Ka

Bunkei

1. Jisho o kashite kudasai.
2. Lee-san wa ima tabako o sutte imasu.

Kaiwa

Mise no hito:	Irasshaimase.
Lee:	Tēpu-rekōdā o misete kudasai.
Mise no hito:	Iroiro arimasu ga, donna tēpu-rekōdā ga ii desu ka.
Lee:	Chiisai no o kudasai.
Mise no hito:	Kono kasetto wa dō desu ka.
Lee:	Sore wa ikura desu ka.
Mise no hito:	2-man-en desu.
Lee:	Dewa, sore o kudasai.

Reibun

1. Motto yukkuri itte kudasai.

2. Sumimasen ga, shio o totte kudasai.
    —Hai, dōzo.

3. Slamet-san wa ima nani o shite imasu ka.
    —Heya de ongaku o kiite imasu.

4. Jikan ga arimasen kara, isoide kudasai.
    —Chotto matte kudasai.
      Lee-san ga mada kimasen.
    Lee-san wa nani o shite imasu ka.
    —Robii de kaisha no hito to hanashite imasu.

5. Ame ga futte imasu ne.
    Takushii o yobimashō ka.
    —Hai, yonde kudasai.

Renshū A

1. Te-kei

Dai I Gurūpu

ka	i	te
ka	ki	masu
ki	ki	masu
hatara	ki	masu
*i	ki	masu
i	t	te
iso	i	de
iso	gi	masu
no	n	de
no	mi	masu
yasu	mi	masu
yo	mi	masu
yo	n	de
yo	bi	masu
aso	bi	masu

to	t	te
to	ri	masu
ki	ri	masu
oku	ri	masu
ma	t	te
ma	chi	masu
ta	chi	masu
ka	t	te
ka	i	masu
su	i	masu
i	i	masu
ka	shi	te
ka	shi	masu
da	shi	masu
hana	shi	masu

Dai II Gurūpu

tabe	te
tabe	masu
ne	masu
oshie	masu
mi	masu
oki	masu
i	masu

Dai III Gurūpu

ki	te
ki	masu
benkyō-shi	te
benkyō-shi	masu
jisshū-shi	masu
kengaku-shi	masu

2.

1)

Jisho o	kashi	te
Shio o	tot	te
Takushii o	yon	de
Tēpu-rekōdā o	mise	te
Namae o	kai	te
Heya ni	hait	te
Koko e	ki	te

kudasai.

2)

Lee-san wa ima

tabako o	sut	te
ongaku o	kii	te
tomodachi to	hanashi	te
denwa o	kake	te
hito o	mat	te
kodomo to	ason	de

imasu.

nani o	shi	te

..... ka.

Renshū B

1. 1) Rei: <u>Uketsuke</u> e kite kudasai.
        (kyōshitsu, shokudō, watashi no heya, jimusho, koko)
    2) Rei: <u>Shashin</u> o misete kudasai.
        (tegami, shatsu, hon, pasupōto, nōto, tēpu-rekōdā)
    3) Rei: <u>Haizara</u> o totte kudasai.
        (matchi, supana, jisho, kagi, shio, satō)

2. Rei: kakimasu — kaite

1) machimasu —	6) kimasu —	11) kaimasu —
2) kakemasu —	7) okimasu —	12) ikimasu —
3) hanashimasu —	8) yobimasu —	13) kirimasu —
4) suimasu —	9) isogimasu —	14) iimasu —
5) kekkon-shimasu —	10) yasumimasu —	15) tsukurimasu —

3. Chāto 5

    1) Rei: (gohan o tabemasu) — Gohan o tabete kudasai.
                                    6) (rekōdo o kikimasu)
    2) (hana o kaimasu)   7) (hon o yomimasu)
    3) (tabako o suimasu)   8) (tegami o kakimasu)
    4) (kōhii o nomimasu)   9) (terebi o mimasu)
    5) (shashin o torimasu)   10) (Nihon-go o benkyō-shimasu)

4. Chāto 7

    1) Rei: (denwa o kakemasu) — Denwa o kakete kudasai.
    2) (takushii o yobimasu)
    3) (10-ji ni nemasu)
    4) (isogimasu)
    5) (uchi e kaerimasu)
    6) (heya de yasumimasu)
    7) (shatsu o sentaku-shimasu)
    8) (rajio o shūri-shimasu)
    9) (Nihon-go de hanashimasu)

5. Rei: Jikan ga arimasen kara, (isogimasu)
        —Jikan ga arimasen kara, isoide kudasai.

    1) Yoku wakarimasen kara, mō ichido (iimasu) —
    2) Ashita shiken ga arimasu kara, konban (benkyō-shimasu) —
    3) Ima okane ga arimasen kara, sukoshi (kashimasu) —
    4) Anata ni tegami o kakimasu kara, jūsho o (oshiemasu) —
    5) 8-ji ni Sentā o demasu kara, 7-ji han ni (kimasu) —
    6) Ima ikimasu kara, chotto (machimasu) —
    7) Ame ga futte imasu kara, takushii de (ikimasu) —

6. Chāto 5

    1) Rei: (gohan o tabemasu) — gohan o tabete imasu
    2) (hana o kaimasu)
    3) (tabako o suimasu)
    4) (kōhii o nomimasu)
    5) (shashin o torimasu)
    6) (rekōdo o kikimasu)
    7) (hon o yomimasu)
    8) (tegami o kakimasu)
    9) (terebi o mimasu)
   10) (Nihon-go o benkyō-shimasu)

7. Rei: tomodachi to hanashimasu
        —tomodachi to hanashite imasu

    1) basu o machimasu —
    2) heya de nemasu —
    3) ame ga furimasu —
    4) shatsu o sentaku-shimasu —
    5) tomodachi to sanpo-shimasu —
    6) Nihon-go o oshiemasu —
    7) niwa de asobimasu —
    8) jimusho de hatarakimasu —
    9) denwa o kakemasu —
   10) Kimura-san ni naraimasu —

Mondai

I. Rei: Gohan ⌈ o ⌉ (tabemasu—tabete kudasai).
   1. Shokudō ⌈ ⌉ terebi ⌈ ⌉ (mimasu—).
   2. 6-ji han ⌈ ⌉ (okimasu—).
   3. Shio ⌈ ⌉ (torimasu—).
   4. 5-ji han ⌈ ⌉ takushii ⌈ ⌉ (yobimasu—).
   5. Supana ⌈ ⌉ penchi ⌈ ⌉ rajio ⌈ ⌉
     (shūri-shimasu—).
   6. Kono nimotsu ⌈ ⌉ Indo ⌈ ⌉ (okurimasu —).
   7. Watashi ⌈ ⌉ enpitsu ⌈ ⌉ (kashimasu —).
   8. Kaiwa ⌈ ⌉ zenbu (oboemasu —).
   9. Kyōshitsu ⌈ ⌉ (hairimasu —).
  10. Anata no uchi ⌈ ⌉ denwa-bangō ⌈ ⌉ (oshiemasu —).

II. Rei: Jikan ga arimasen kara, (isoide) kudasai.
   1. Anata no namae ga wakarimasen.
     Namae o ( ) kudasai.
   2. ( ) kara, chotto matte kudasai.
   3. Anata wa netsu ga arimasu ne.
     Heya de ( ) kudasai.
   4. ( ) kara, okane o kashite kudasai.
   5. Anata no okusan no shashin o mitai desu.
     Okusan no shashin o ( ) kudasai.

III. 1. Anata wa ima tabako o sutte imasu ka.
    2. Ima doko de benkyō-shite imasu ka.
    3. Anata wa ima nani o shite imasu ka.
    4. Ima ame ga futte imasu ka.
    5 Anata wa ima rajio o kiite imasu ka.

Dai 15 Ka

Bunkei

1. Kono tēpu-rekōdā o tsukatte mo ii desu.
2. Watashi wa ii kamera o motte imasu.

Kaiwa

Rao: Ali-san, ano onna no hito o shitte imasu ka.

Ali: Iie, shirimasen.

　　　Dare desu ka.

Rao: Suzuki-san desu yo.

　　　Sentā no chikaku ni sunde imasu.

Ali: Kireina hito desu ne.

　　　Dokushin desu ka.

Rao: Iie, mō kekkon-shite imasu.

Reibun

1. Ii desu ka.
   —Hai, ii desu. (kekkō desu.)
   —Iie, ikemasen. (dame desu.)

2. Mō kaette mo ii desu ka.
   —Hai, kaette mo ii desu.
   —Iie, ikemasen.

3. Anata wa kasa o motte imasu ka.
   —Iie, motte imasen.
   Dewa, watashi no o kashimashō ka.
   —Hai, kashite kudasai.

4. Anata wa doko ni sunde imasu ka.
   —Kenshū Sentā ni sunde imasu.
   Soredewa, Indo no Rao-san o shitte imasu ka.
   —Hai, shitte imasu.
   —Iie, shirimasen.

5. Anata no kaisha wa nani o tsukutte imasu ka.
   —Terebi o tsukutte imasu.

6. Doko de kitte ya fūtō o utte imasu ka.
   —Uketsuke de utte imasu.

7. Kuraku narimashita ne.
   Denki o tsukemashō ka.
   —Hai, tsukete kudasai.

Renshū A

1.

Taipu o	tsukat	te
Tabako o	sut	te
Mado o	ake	te
Shashin o	tot	te
Sake o	non	de
Uchi e	kaet	te
Pen de	kai	te
Isu ni	suwat	te

mo ii desu.

2. Watashi wa

kamera o	motte
Sentā ni	sunde
Tanom-san o	shitte

imasu.

3. Heya no naka ga

samu	ku
akaru	ku
kirei	ni
shizuka	ni

narimashita.

4.

Yoru
12-ji
Sensei

ni narimashita.

Renshū B

1. Chāto 8

    1) Rei: (mado o akemasu) — Mado o akete kudasai.
    2) (mado o shimemasu)
    3) (terebi o tsukemasu)
    4) (terebi o keshimasu)
    5) (Ali-san ni hon o agemasu)
    6) (Rao-san kara hon o moraimasu)
    7) (haizara o okimasu)
    8) (haizara o torimasu)

2. Rei: Takushii o yobimashō ka. — Hai, yonde kudasai.
    1) Doa o akemashō ka. —
    2) Kasa o kashimashō ka. —
    3) Mō ichido iimashō ka. —
    4) Tetsudaimashō ka. —
    5) Denwa-bangō o oshiemashō ka. —
    6) Dare ni hanashimashō ka. (Tanaka-san) —
    7) Nan-ji ni koko e kimashō ka. (6-ji han) —
    8) Kusuri o agemashō ka. —*

3. Rei: ikimasu — itte mo ii desu
    1) ashita kimasu —
    2) kaisha o yasumimasu —
    3) heya ni hairimasu —
    4) tabako o suimasu —
    5) pen de kakimasu —
    6) Ei-go de hanashimasu —
    7) soto e demasu —
    8) denki o keshimasu —

4. Chāto 8

    1) Rei: (Mado o akete mo) ii desu.

	5) ( ) ii desu.
2) ( ) ii desu.	6) ( ) ii desu.
3) ( ) ii desu.	7) ( ) ii desu.
4) ( ) ii desu.	8) ( ) ii desu.

5. Chāto 5

   1) Rei: koko de — Koko de gohan o tabete mo ii desu ka.
                                  6) koko de —
   2) koko de —   7) koko de —
   3) koko de —   8) koko de —
   4) koko de —   9) koko de —
   5) koko de —   10) koko de —

6. 1) Rei: Anata wa kamera o motte imasu ka.
          (jidōsha, tokei, rajio, jisho, kasa, pasupōto)
   2) Rei: Anata wa doko ni sunde imasu ka.
          (Tanaka-san, anata no kazoku, anata no okusan)
   3) Rei: Anata wa Lee-san o shitte imasu ka.
          (ano hito, ano hito no okusan, kaisha no denwa-bangō, Rao-san no jūsho)

7. Rei: Kaette mo ii desu ka. (iie) — Iie, ikemasen.
   1) Koko de shashin o totte mo ii desu ka. (iie) —
   2) Kono taipu o tsukatte mo ii desu ka. (hai) —
   3) Rao-san o shitte imasu ka. (iie) —
   4) Shokudō de o-sake o nonde mo ii desu ka. (iie) —
   5) Anata wa ii kamera o motte imasu ka. (hai) —
   6) Konban denwa o kakete mo ii desu ka. (hai) —
   7) Anata no kazoku wa Nihon ni sunde imasu ka. (iie) —
   8) Heya ni haitte mo ii desu ka. (hai) —
   9) Tanaka-san o shitte imasu ka. (hai) —
   10) Kono katarogu o moratte mo ii desu ka. (iie) —

8. Rei 1: takai desu — takaku narimasu
   Rei 2: yūmei desu — yūmeini narimasu
   1) hayai desu —   6) shizuka desu —
   2) kurai desu —   7) atsui desu —
   3) kirei desu —   8) byōki desu —
   4) jōzu desu —   9) sensei desu —
   5) ōkii desu —   10) ii desu —

Mondai

I. Rei: Namae o (kakimasu—kaite) kudasai.
1. Shinbun o (yomimasu—   ) imasu.
2. Ocha o (nomimasu—   ) tai desu.
3. Eiga o (mimasu—   ) ni ikimashō.
4. Mō (hatarakimasu—   ) takunai desu.
5. Shashin o (torimasu—   ) mo ii desu.
6. Denki no (jisshū-shimasu—   ) ni kimashita.
7. Koko de tabako o (suimasu—   ) mo ii desu ka.
8. Gohan o takusan (tabemasu—   ) kudasai.
9. Nihon-go de (hanashimasu—   ) mashō.
10. Chotto (tetsudaimasu—   ) kudasai.

II. Rei: Takushii o yobimashō ka. — Hai, yonde kudasai.
1. Haizara o torimashō ka. —
2. Mō ichido iimashō ka. —
3. Denwa-bangō o kakimashō ka. —
Rei: (Nan-ji ni denwa o kakemashō ka.)
        —San-ji ni denwa o kakete kudasai.
4. (   ) — Lee-san o yonde kudasai.
5. (   ) — Pen de kaite kudasai.
6. (   ) — Ringo o itsutsu katte kudasai.

III. 1. Kyōshitsu de tabako o sutte mo ii desu ka.
2. Anata no kazoku wa doko ni sunde imasu ka.
3. Heya de o-sake o nonde mo ii desu ka.
4. Anata no kaisha no denwa-bangō o shitte imasu ka.
5. Anata wa jidōsha o motte imasu ka.
6. Anata no kuni de nan-sai kara tabako o sutte mo ii desu ka.
7. Indo no onna no hito wa nani o kite imasu ka.
8. Anata wa kekkon-shite imasu ka.
9. Uketsuke de nani o utte imasu ka.
10. Anata wa kuni de donna shigoto o shite imasu ka.

— 93 —

Dai 16 Ka

Bunkei

1. Asa okite, gohan o tabete, kyōshitsu e kimashita.
2. Kono ringo wa ōkikute, oishii desu.
3. Anata wa Indo-jin de, watashi wa Nihon-jin desu.
4. Shigoto ga owatte kara, eiga o mimashita.

Kaiwa

Slamet: Sumimasen ga, chotto purēyā o kashite kudasai.
Tanaka: Dōzo. Kore wa karukute, oto ga ii desu.
Slamet: Ashita made tsukatte mo ii desu ka.
Tanaka: Iie, sore wa komarimasu.
         Watashi mo purēyā ga irimasu.
Slamet: Jā, ato de kaeshi ni kimasu.

Reibun

1. Kinō Tōkyō e ikimashita ka.
   —Hai, kōgi ga owatte kara, sugu ikimashita.
   Tōkyō e itte, nani o shimashita ka.
   —Ginza e itte, tomodachi ni atte, sorekara issho ni biiru o nomimashita.

2. Ano hito wa dare desu ka.
   —Rao-san desu.
   Indo-jin de, Ōsaka-kagaku no kenshūsei desu.

3. Arora-san wa donna hito desu ka.
   —Wakakute, kirei de, atama ga ii desu.

4. Kōgi ga owatte kara, nani o shimasu ka.
   —Heya e kaette, yasumimasu.

Renshū A

1.
Heya e kaet te	yasumimasu.	
Niwa e de te	shashin o torimasu.	
Basu ni not te	kaerimashita.	

Asa oki te	gohan o tabe te	kyōshitsu e kimasu.
Ginza e it te	tomodachi ni at te	eiga o mimashita.

2. Ano hito wa
wakaku te	kirei desu.
atama ga yoku te	hansamu desu.
kirei de	atama ga ii desu.
hansamu de	okane ga arimasu.

3.
Rao-san wa Indo-jin de,	Lee-san wa Chūgoku-jin	desu.
Ali-san wa kenshūsei	senmon wa denki	
Koko wa jimusho	soko wa uketsuke	

4.
Shigoto ga owat te kara,	eiga o mimasu.	
Tegami o kai te	nemashita.	
Denki o keshi te	heya o demasu.	
Nihon e ki te	kekkon-shimashita.	
10-pun arui te	densha ni norimasu.	

5. Arora-san wa
me	ga	kirei	desu.
se		takai	
kami		nagai	
hana		takai	
atama		ii	

Renshū B

1. Chāto 9

   1) Rei: (asa 6-ji ni okimasu)
      —Asa 6-ji ni okite kudasai.
   2) (gohan o tabemasu)
   3) (kyōshitsu e kimasu)
   4) (heya ni hairimasu)
   5) (mado o akemasu)
   6) (heya o sōji-shimasu)
   7) (Tōkyō e ikimasu)
   8) (tomodachi ni aimasu)
   9) (issho ni sanpo-shimasu)
   10) (Tōkyō de densha ni norimasu)
   11) (Yokohama de densha o orimasu)
   12) (kōjō made arukimasu)

2. Rei: (Ginza e ikimashita) (tomodachi ni aimashita) (issho ni kaimono-
   shimashita) — Ginza e itte, tomodachi ni atte, issho ni kaimono-
   shimashita.
   1) (heya e kaerimasu) (sukoshi yasumimasu) (pinpon-shimasu) —
   2) (tegami o kakimashita) (benkyō-shimashita) (nemashita) —
   3) (robii e ikimasu) (isu ni suwarimasu) (hon o yomimasu) —
   4) (mado o shimemasu) (denki o keshimasu) (heya o demasu) —
   5) (denwa o kakemashita) (takushii o yobimashita) (tomodachi no uchi e
   ikimashita) —

3. Chāto 9

   Rei: (1) to (2) to (3) — Asa 6-ji ni okite, gohan o tabete, kyōshitsu e
   kimasu.
   1) (4) to (5) to (6) —
   2) (7) to (8) to (9) —
   3) (10) to (11) to (12) —

4. Rei 1: (kono ringo wa yasui desu) (oishii desu)
    —Kono ringo wa yasukute, oishii desu.

    Rei 2: (watashi wa Nihon-jin desu) (anata wa Indo-jin desu)
    —Watashi wa Nihon-jin de, anata wa Indo-jin desu.

    1) (ano onna no hito wa wakai desu) (kirei desu) —
    2) (watashi no kamera wa chiisai desu) (karui desu) —
    3) (kōjō-kengaku wa omoshiroi desu) (yaku ni tachimasu) —
    4) (kono heya wa akarui desu) (hiroi desu) (kirei desu) —
    5) (Fujisan wa takai desu) (kirei desu) (yūmei desu) —
    6) (ano hito wa atama ga ii desu) (hansamu desu) (okane ga arimasu) —
    7) (kono tēpu-rekōdā wa kantan desu) (benri desu) (yasui desu) —
    8) (ano hito wa Firipin-jin desu) (namae wa Garcia-san desu) —
    9) (Abebe-san wa Ōsaka-kagaku no kenshūsei desu) (senmon wa kagaku
       desu) —
    10) (gozen wa Nihon-go desu) (gogo wa kōgi desu) (tokidoki kōjō-kengaku
        ni ikimasu) —

5. Rei: (shigoto ga owarimasu) (eiga o mimasu)
    —Shigoto ga owatte kara, eiga o mimasu.

    1) (kōgi ga owarimasu) (kaimono-shimasu) —
    2) (10-pun yasumimasu) (benkyō-shimasu) —
    3) (katarogu o mimashita) (kaimashita) —
    4) (densha ga tomarimasu) (orite kudasai) —
    5) (10-pun arukimashita) (chikatetsu ni norimashita) —
    6) (uketsuke ni kagi o kaeshimasu)(Sentā o demasu) —

6. Chāto 10

    1) Rei: (shinbun o yomimasu) (tegami o kakimasu)
       —Shinbun o yonde kara, tegami o kakimasu.
    2) (sentaku-shimashita) (pinpon-shimashita)
    3) (benkyō-shimasu) (asobimasu)
    4) (okane o haraimasu) (eiga o mimasu)
    5) (denki o keshimasu) (heya o demasu)
    6) (kekkon-shimashita) (Nihon e kimashita)

Mondai

I. 1. Ginza e (ikimasu—   ), tomodachi ni (aimasu—   ),
       sorekara issho ni biiru o nomimashita.

   2. Gohan o (tabemasu—   ), kusuri o (nomimasu—   )
       nete kudasai.

   3. Arora-san wa (wakai desu—   ), (kirei desu—   ), atama ga
       ii desu.

   4. Kono tēpu-rekōdā wa (karui desu—   ),
       (kantan desu—   ), benri desu.

   5. Kyō wa (nichi-yōbi desu—   ), hima desu.

II. 1. Ame ☐ futte imasu kara, takushii ☐ yonde kudasai.

   2. Atama ☐ itai desu kara, gohan ☐ tabete kara, nemasu.

   3. Gohan no jikan desu kara, shokudō ☐ itte kudasai.

   4. 5-ji ☐ kōgi ☐ owatte kara, sanpo-shimasu.

   5. Nihon ☐ jisshū-shimasu kara, 5-shūkan Nihon-go ☐ benkyō-
       shimasu.

III. 1. Anata wa hirugohan o tabete kara, nani o shimasu ka.
       (—te, —te, o tsukatte kudasai.)

   2. Heya e kaette, nani o shimasu ka.

   3. Kuni e kaette kara, doko de hatarakimasu ka.

   4. Anata no sensei wa donna hito desu ka.
       (—kute, —de, o tsukatte kudasai.)

   5. Nihon wa dō desu ka. (—kute, —de, o tsukatte kudasai.)

   6. 12-ji made benkyō-shite kara, donokurai yasumimasu ka.

   7. Anata wa Nihon e kite kara, donna tokoro e ikimashita ka.

   8. Ashita Nihon-go o benkyō-shite kara kōgi o kikimasu ka, kōjō o kengaku-
       shimasu ka.

   9. Anata wa bangohan o tabete kara benkyō-shimasu ka, benkyō-shite
       kara gohan o tabemasu ka.

  10. Donokurai Nihon-go o naratte kara, kōjō de jisshū-shimasu ka.

Dai 17 Ka

Bunkei

1. Watashi o wasurenai de kudasai.
2. Kenshūsei wa mainichi benkyō-shinakereba narimasen.
                    (benkyō-shinai to ikemasen.)
3. Ima okane o harawanakute mo ii desu.

Kaiwa

Lee: Gomen kudasai.
          Tanaka-san wa imasu ka.

Tanaka: Yā, Lee-san, shibaraku desu ne.
          Kega wa naorimashita ka.

Lee: Hai, mō daijōbu desu kara, shinpai-shinai de kudasai.

Tanaka: Sore wa yokatta desu ne.

Lee: Mō 9-ji desu ne. Kaeranakereba narimasen.

Tanaka: Jā, karada ni ki o tsukete kudasai.

Lee: Hai, arigatō gozaimasu.

Reibun

1. Kōhii ni satō o irenai de kudasai.

2. Kōjō de Nihon-go o hanasanakereba narimasen ka.
   —Hai, hanasanakereba narimasen.
   —Iie, hanasanakute mo ii desu.

3. Nan-ji ni Sentā e kaeranakereba narimasen ka.
   —8-ji ni kaeranakereba narimasen.

4. Sentā de kutsu o nuganakereba narimasen ka.
   —Iie, nuganakute mo ii desu.

5. Kono suitchi ni sawaranai de kudasai.
   —Dōshite desu ka.
   Abunai desu kara.
   —Wakarimashita. Ki o tsukemasu.

Renshū A

1. Nai-kei

Dai I Gurūpu

ka	ka	nai
ka	ki	masen
ki	ki	masen
hatara	ki	masen
i	ki	masen
nu	ga	nai
nu	gi	masen
iso	gi	masen
yo	ma	nai
yo	mi	masen
no	mi	masen
yasu	mi	masen
yo	ba	nai
yo	bi	masen
aso	bi	masen

to	ra	nai
to	ri	masen
ki	ri	masen
shi	ri	masen
ma	ta	nai
ma	chi	masen
ta	chi	masen
mo	chi	masen
ka	wa	nai
ka	i	masen
su	i	masen
i	i	masen
ka	sa	nai
ka	shi	masen
da	shi	masen

Dai II Gurūpu

tabe	nai
tabe	masen
wasure	masen
ire	masen
tsuke	masen
mi	masen
oki	masen
i	masen

Dai III Gurūpu

ko	nai
ki	masen
benkyō-shi	nai
benkyō-shi	masen
shinpai-shi	masen
kaimono-shi	masen

2.

1)

Watashi o	wasure	nai	de kudasai.
Suitchi ni	sawara	nai	
Koko e	ko	nai	
Ano hito ni	hanasa	nai	

2)

Nihon-go o	benkyō-shi	nakereba	narimasen.
Uchi e	kaera	nakereba	
Kaisha e	ika	nakereba	
Pasupōto o	mise	nakereba	

3)

Kono kotoba o	oboe	nakute	mo ii desu.
Kutsu o	nuga	nakute	
Kyōshitsu e	ko	nakute	
Ano hito ni	iwa	nakute	

Renshū B

1. 1) Rei: <u>Nihon-go</u> o wasurenai de kudasai.
      (kono kotoba, jūsho, pasupōto, kamera, denwa-**bangō**)
   2) Rei: <u>Koko</u> e konai de kudasai.
      (kyōshitsu, jimusho, watashi no heya, watashi no **uchi**)
   3) Rei: <u>Sensei</u> ni iwanai de kudasai.
      (ano hito, Ali-san, watashi no koibito, jimusho no **hito**)

2. Rei: ikimasu — ikanai

1) arukimasu —	6) mochimasu —	11) motte kimasu —
2) nugimasu —	7) waraimasu —	12) sentaku-shimasu —
3) nomimasu —	8) kaeshimasu —	13) tsukaimasu —
4) asobimasu —	9) wasuremasu —	14) tomemasu —
5) torimasu —	10) orimasu —	15) keshimasu —

3. Rei: shinpai-shimasu — Shinpai-shinai de kudasai.
   1) Ei-go o hanashimasu —
   2) kikai ni sawarimasu —
   3) yoru osoku sentaku-shimasu —
   4) koko de tabako o suimasu —
   5) watashi no heya ni hairimasu —
   6) kono denwa o tsukaimasu —
   7) pasupōto o nakushimasu —
   8) waraimasu —
   9) koko ni jidōsha o tomemasu —

4. Chāto 8

   1) Rei: mado o — Mado o akenai de kudasai.

	6) Rao-san kara hon o —
2) mado o —	7) tsukue no ue ni haizara o —
3) terebi o —	8) tsukue no ue kara haizara o —
4) terebi o —	9) hako no naka ni kagi o (iremasu) —
5) Ali-san ni hon o —	10) hako no naka kara kagi o (dashimasu) —

5. Rei : okane o haraimasu — Okane o harawanakereba narimasen.
   1) maiban benkyō-shimasu —
   2) kusuri o nomimasu —
   3) mainichi hatarakimasu —
   4) 6-ji ni okimasu —
   5) byōin e ikimasu —
   6) ki o tsukemasu —

6. Rei : kaisha e ikimasu — Kaisha e ikanakute mo ii desu.
   1) repōto o dashimasu —
   2) kōhii ni satō o iremasu —
   3) pasupōto o motte kimasu —
   4) ima okane o haraimasu —
   5) ano hikōki ni norimasu —
   6) kotoba o zenbu oboemasu —

7. Chāto 7
   1) Rei : Ashita yasumimasu kara, kaisha ni
      —denwa o kakenakereba narimasen.
   2) Ame ga futte imasu kara, takushii o —
   3) Ashita hayaku okimasu kara, 10-ji ni —
   4) Jikan ga arimasen kara, —
   5) 9-ji desu kara, uchi e —
   6) Anata wa byōki desu kara, heya de —
   7) Atarashii shatsu ga arimasen kara, —
   8) Kono rajio wa oto ga warui desu kara, —
   9) Ano hito wa Ei-go ga wakarimasen kara, —

8. Rei : Byōin e ikanakereba narimasen ka. (iie)
      —Iie, ikanakute mo ii desu.
   1) Kōjō de Nihon-go o hanasanakereba narimasen ka. (hai) —
   2) Ima okane o harawanakereba narimasen ka. (iie) —
   3) Koko de kutsu o nuganakereba narimasen ka. (iie) —
   4) Pasupōto o misenakereba narimasen ka. (hai) —
   5) Ashita mo konakereba narimasen ka. (iie) —
   6) Konban repōto o dasanakereba narimasen ka. (hai) —

Mondai

I. Rei 1: Mainichi Nihon-go o (hanashimasu—hanasanakereba narimasen).
    Rei 2: Nichi-yōbi desu kara, kyōshitsu e (kimasen—konakute mo ii desu).
1. Byōki wa naorimashita kara, (hatarakimasu—   ).
2. Watashi ga okane o haraimasu kara, anata wa (haraimasen—   ).
3. Daijōbu desu kara, (shinpai-shimasen—   ).
4. Anata wa Nihon-go ga mada heta desu kara, motto Nihon-go o (benkyō-shimasu—   ).

II. Rei: Denki o (keshimasu—keshite) kudasai.
           (keshimasu—kesa) nai de kudasai.
           (keshimasu—keshite) mo ii desu.
1. Shashin o (torimasu—   ) mo ii desu.
           (torimasu—   ) kudasai.
           (torimasu—   ) nakereba narimasen.
2. Tabako o (suimasu—   ) imasu.
           (suimasu—   ) nai de kudasai.
           (suimasu—   ) tai desu.

III.
1. Anata wa maiasa nan-ji ni okinakereba narimasen ka.
2. Anata no kaisha no hito wa 1-shūkan ni nan-nichi hatarakanakereba narimasen ka.
3. Kaisha ni repōto o dasanakereba narimasen ka.
4. Mainichi sentaku-shinakereba narimasen ka.
5. Anata wa kōjō de donokurai jisshū-shinakereba narimasen ka.
6. Anata wa doko no kōjō de jisshū-shinakereba narimasen ka.
7. Itsu kuni e kaeranakereba narimasen ka.
8. Anata no kuni ni tegami o dashimasu.
    Ikura no kitte o kawanakereba narimasen ka.
9. Kuni e kaette kara, doko de hatarakanakereba narimasen ka.
10. Gaikoku e ikimasu.
    Nani o motte ikanakereba narimasen ka.

Dai 18 Ka

Bunkei

1. Watashi wa jidōsha no unten ga dekimasu.
2. Watashi wa Nihon-go o sukoshi hanasu koto ga dekimasu.
3. Kochira e kuru mae ni, denwa o kakete kudasai.

Kaiwa

Cortez: Moshi moshi.
Katō-san wa irasshaimasu ka.
Katō-san no okusan: Ima imasen ga, donata desu ka.
Cortez: Watashi wa Mekishiko no Cortez desu.
Ashita kuni e kaerimasu ga, kaeru mae ni,
Katō-san ni aitai desu.
Okusan: Shujin wa kinō ryokō ni ikimashita.
Cortez: Sō desu ka. Sore wa zannen desu.
Dewa, yoroshiku itte kudasai.
Okusan: Wakarimashita.
Dōzo o-genki de.

Reibun

1. Anata wa **Nihon-go** ga dekimasu ka.
   —Hai, sukoshi dekimasu.

2. Anata wa terebi no koshō o naosu koto ga dekimasu ka.
   —Iie, [naosu koto ga] dekimasen.

3. Neru mae ni, nani o shimasu ka.
   —Shawā o abimasu.

4. Anata wa itsu kekkon-shimashita ka.
   —Nihon e kuru sukoshi mae ni, kekkon-shimashita.

5. Nihon e kuru mae ni, Nihon-go o benkyō-shimashita ka.
   —Iie, zenzen shimasendeshita.
   Dewa, itsu kara, benkyō o hajimemashita ka.
   —Nihon e kite kara, sugu hajimemashita.

Renshū A

1. Jisho-kei

Dai I Gurūpu

i	ku	
i	ki	masu
ka	ki	masu
aru	ki	masu
iso	gu	
iso	gi	masu
oyo	gi	masu
nu	gi	masu
yo	mu	
yo	mi	masu
yasu	mi	masu
no	mi	masu
yo	bu	
yo	bi	masu
aso	bi	masu

to	ru	
to	ri	masu
hai	ri	masu
suwa	ri	masu
ma	tsu	
ma	chi	masu
ta	chi	masu
ka	u	
ka	i	masu
hara	i	masu
tsuka	i	masu
ka	su	
ka	shi	masu
ke	shi	masu
nao	shi	masu

Dai II Gurūpu

tabe	ru
tabe	masu
de	masu
mise	masu
oboe	masu
oki	masu
ori	masu
deki	masu

Dai III Gurūpu

ku	ru
	ki	masu
benkyō-su	ru
benkyō-shi	masu
unten-shi	masu
pinpon-shi	masu

2. 1) Watashi wa

pinpon
Nihon-go
dansu
jidōsha no unten

ga dekimasu.

2) Watashi wa

o-sake o nomu
rajio o naosu
kanji o yomu
jidōsha o unten-suru

koto ga dekimasu.

3)

Taberu	te o araimashō.
Jisshū ni iku	Nihon-go o benkyō-shimasu.
Nihon e kuru	kekkon-shimashita.
Heya ni hairu	nokku-shinakereba narimasen.

mae ni,

— 108 —

Renshū B

1. 1) Rei: Watashi wa <u>tenisu</u> ga dekimasu.
      (pinpon, dansu, Nihon-go, kuruma no unten, erebētā no shūri)
   2) Rei: <u>Ei-go</u> o hanasu koto ga dekimasu.
      (Nihon-go, Chūgoku-go, Supein-go)
   3) Rei: <u>Terebi</u> no koshō o naosu koto ga dekimasu.
      (rajio, tokei, kamera, kuruma, denwa)

2. Rei: kakimasu — kaku

1) hatarakimasu —	6) tachimasu —	11) kimasu —
2) oyogimasu —	7) aimasu —	12) unten-shimasu —
3) yasumimasu —	8) hanashimasu —	13) naoshimasu —
4) yobimasu —	9) hajimemasu —	14) machimasu —
5) hairimasu —	10) dekimasu —	15) suimasu —

3. 1) Rei: Sentā de <u>okane o kaeru</u> koto ga dekimasu.
      ⎧ kitte o kaimasu, denwa o kakemasu, tegami o dashimasu, ⎫
      ⎩ sentaku-shimasu, gohan o tabemasu, eiga o mimasu ⎭
   2) Rei: Watashi wa mada <u>Nihon-go o hanasu</u> koto ga dekimasen.
      ⎧ kanji o yomimasu, hitori de Tōkyō e ikimasu, ⎫
      ⎪ Nihon-go de denwa o kakemasu, anata o wasuremasu, ⎪
      ⎩ sake o nomimasu ⎭

4. Rei 1: kanji o yomimasu — Kanji o yomu koto ga dekimasu.
   Rei 2: hiragana o kakimasen — Hiragana o kaku koto ga dekimasen.
   1) Yokohama kara shinkansen ni norimasu —
   2) Nihon-go de uta o utaimasen —
   3) ginkō de okane o karimasu —
   4) gitā o hikimasen —
   5) 1000-mētoru gurai oyogimasu —
   6) uketsuke de okane o kaemasu —
   7) jidōsha o shūri-shimasu —
   8) ano hito to kekkon-shimasen —
   9) piano o hikimasu —
   10) jimusho no taipu o tsukaimasen —

5. Rei: Hashi de taberu koto ga dekimasu ka.
    (hai) — Hai, dekimasu.

    1) Mō ichido Nihon e kuru koto ga dekimasu ka.
       (hai) —
    2) Kono kagi de doa o akeru koto ga dekimasu ka.
       (iie) —
    3) Nihon-go o oshieru koto ga dekimasu ka.
       (iie, zenzen) —
    4) Nihon-go o hanasu koto ga dekimasu ka.
       (hai, sukoshi) —
    5) Jidōsha o unten-suru koto ga dekimasu ka.
       (hai, mochiron) —

6. Rei: doa o akemasu, nokku-shimasu
        —Doa o akeru mae ni, nokku-shimasu.

    1) kōhii o nomimasu, satō o iremasu —
    2) benkyō o hajimemasu, shiken o shimashō —
    3) Nihon e kimashita, Nihon-go o benkyō-shimashita —
    4) gohan o tabemasu, kusuri o nonde kudasai —
    5) jisshū ni ikimasu, Nihon-go o benkyō-shimasu —
    6) tomodachi ni aimasu, denwa o kakemasu —
    7) kekkon-shimashita, jidōsha o kaimashita —

7. Chāto 10

    1) Rei: (tegami o kakimasu) (shinbun o yomimasu)
           —Tegami o kaku mae ni, shinbun o yomimasu.
    2) (pinpon-shimasu) (sentaku-shimasu)
    3) (asobimasu) (benkyō-shimasu)
    4) (eiga o mimasu) (okane o haraimasu)
    5) (heya o demasu) (denki o keshimasu)
    6) (Nihon e kimashita) (kekkon-shimashita)
    7) (unten-shimasu) (naoshimasu)
    8) (heya ni hairimasu) (doa o nokku-shimasu)
    9) (nemasu) (shawā o abimasu)
    10) (gohan o tabemasu) (te o araimasu)

Mondai

I. 1. (nemasu—   ) mae ni, shawā o abimasu.
    2. (benkyō-shimasu—   ) kara, tegami o kakimashita.
    3. Kōjō e (ikimasu—   ) mae ni, Nihon-go o benkyō-shimasu.
    4. (dekakemasu—   ) mae ni, denwa o kakemasu.
    5. Kuni e (kaerimasu—   ) kara, tegami o kakimasu.

II. 1. Niwa de (asobimasu—   ) imasu.
            (asobimasu—   ) nai de kudasai.
            (asobimasu—   ) mo ii desu.
    2. Nihon-go o (hanashimasu—   ) koto ga dekimasu.
            (hanashimasu—   ) kudasai.
            (hanashimasu—   ) nakute mo ii desu.
    3. Koko ni (imasu—   ) kudasai.
            (imasu—   ) nakereba narimasen.
            (imasu—   ) tai desu.

III. 1. Anata wa Tai-go o hanasu koto ga dekimasu ka.
     2. Jimusho de okane o kaeru koto ga dekimasu ka.
     3. Anata no kuni de, nan-sai kara jidōsha no unten ga dekimasu ka.
     4. Anata wa tomodachi ni Nihon-go o oshieru koto ga dekimasu ka.
     5. Neru mae ni benkyō-shimasu ka, asa okite kara benkyō-shimasu ka.
     6. Anata wa Nihon e kuru mae ni, Nihon-go o hanasu koto ga dekimashita ka.
     7. Kyōshitsu o deru mae ni, denki o kesanakereba narimasen ka.
     8. Kuni e kaeru mae ni, anata wa nani o kaimasu ka.
     9. Anata wa niku o taberu koto ga dekimasu ka.
     10. Anata wa Nihon-go de uta o utau koto ga dekimasu ka.

Dai 19 Ka

Bunkei

1. Watashi wa Fujisan o mita koto ga arimasu.
2. Basu wa osoi desu kara, densha de itta hō ga ii desu.
3. Anata wa byōki desu kara, soto e denai hō ga ii desu.
4. Gohan o tabeta ato de, pinpon-shimasen ka.

Kaiwa

Tanom:	Moshi moshi, Katō-san ja arimasen ka.
Katō:	Shitsurei desu ga, donata desu ka.
Tanom:	Tai no Tanom desu.
	3-nen mae ni, Bankoku de ichi-do atta koto ga arimasu.
Katō:	Ā, Tanom-san desu ka. Dōmo shitsurei-shimashita.
Tanom:	Iie, kamaimasen.
	Kochira wa Lee-san desu.
	Onaji kaisha de jisshū-shite imasu.
Lee:	Hajimemashite, dōzo yoroshiku.
Katō:	Kochira koso, dōzo yoroshiku.

Reibun

1. Anata wa yuki o mita koto ga arimasu ka.
   —Hai, [mita koto ga] arimasu.
   —Iie, [mita koto ga] arimasen.

2. Ginza e itta koto ga arimasu ka.
   —Hai, 1-kai (ichi-do) arimasu.

3. Kusuri o nonda hō ga ii desu ka.
   —Hai, nonda hō ga ii desu.
   —Iie, nomanai hō ga ii desu.

4. Hirugohan o tabeta ato de, nani o shimasu ka.
   —Kōen e sanpo ni ikimasu.

5. Orientēshon no ato de, Hiroshima no kōjō e ikimasu.

6. Takai desu kara, Ginza de kawanai hō ga ii desu.
   —Soredewa, doko ga ii desu ka.
   Ueno ka Asakusa ga ii desu. Itta koto ga arimasu ka.
   —Iie, zenzen arimasen.

Renshū A

1. Ta-kei

<table>
<tr><th colspan="3" style="text-align:center">Dai I Gurūpu</th><th colspan="3"></th><th colspan="2" style="text-align:center">Dai II Gurūpu</th></tr>
</table>

ka	i	ta		to	t	ta		tabe	ta
ka	ki	mashita		to	ri	mashita		tabe	mashita
aru	ki	mashita		no	ri	mashita		ake	mashita
*i	ki	mashita		koma	ri	mashita		age	mashita
i	t	ta		a	ri	mashita		dekake	mashita
iso	i	da		ma	t	ta		mi	mashita
iso	gi	mashita		ma	chi	mashita		kari	mashita
nu	gi	mashita		ta	chi	mashita		abi	mashita
oyo	gi	mashita		ka	t	ta			

Dai III Gurūpu

yasu	n	da		ka	i	mashita		ki	ta
yasu	mi	mashita		i	i	mashita		ki	mashita
no	mi	mashita		ara	i	mashita			
yo	mi	mashita		hana	shi	ta		benkyō-shi	ta
aso	n	da		hana	shi	mashita		benkyō-shi	mashita
aso	bi	mashita		nao	shi	mashita		kekkon-shi	mashita
yo	bi	mashita		kae	shi	mashita		shūri-shi	mashita

2. 1) Watashi wa

Fujisan o mi	ta
Ginza e it	ta
shinkansen ni not	ta

koto ga arimasu.

2)

Densha de it	ta
Kusuri o non	da
O-sake o yame	ta

hō ga ii desu.

Soto e de	nai
Ginza de kawa	nai
Amari hataraka	nai

3)

Gohan o tabe	ta
Kaisha ga owat	ta
Nara o kenbutsu-shi	ta

ato de,

pinpon-shimasen ka.
eiga o mimashō.
Kyōto e ikimashita.

Renshū B

1. 1) Rei: Watashi wa Fujisan o mita koto ga arimasu.
      (Nihon no eiga, yuki, Tōkyō-tawā, kabuki)
   2) Rei: Watashi wa Kyōto e itta koto ga arimasen.
      (Indo, Nihonjin no uchi, Amerika, Hiroshima)
   3) Rei: Watashi wa 1-kai sukiyaki o tabeta koto ga arimasu.
      (Indo-ryōri, Tai-ryōri, Nihon-ryōri, Chūgoku-ryōri)

2. Rei: taberu — tabeta
1) yasumu —	6) neru —	11) miru —
2) owaru —	7) asobu —	12) iku —
3) au —	8) oyogu —	13) suwaru —
4) matsu —	9) deru —	14) kariru —
5) hanasu —	10) aruku —	15) sōji-suru —

3. Chāto 5
   1) Rei: (sukiyaki) — Sukiyaki o tabeta koto ga arimasu.

	6) (Indo no ongaku)
2) (Ei-go no shinbun)	7) (denki no hon)
3) (Amerika no tabako)	8) (Nihon-go no tegami)
4) (Burajiru no kōhii)	9) (Chūgoku no eiga)
5) (Fujisan no shashin)	10) (Indoneshia-go)

4. Rei 1: yuki o mimasu — Yuki o mita koto ga arimasu.
   Rei 2: Nihon-jin no uchi e ikimasen — Nihon-jin no uchi e itta koto ga
   arimasen.
   1) Kyōto e ikimasu —
   2) Fujisan o mimasu —
   3) ano kasetto o tsukaimasen —
   4) shinkansen ni norimasu —
   5) ano hito to hanashimasen —
   6) Nihon no sake o nomimasen —

5. Rei: Nan-kai Tōkyō e itta koto ga arimasu ka. (3-kai)
      —3-kai arimasu.
   1) Nan-kai shinkansen ni notta koto ga arimasu ka. (ichi-do) —
   2) Nan-kai Nihon no o-sake o nonda koto ga arimasu ka. (3-kai) —
   3) Nan-kai yuki o mita koto ga arimasu ka. (1-kai dake) —
   4) Nan-kai hoteru ni tomatta koto ga arimasu ka. (5-kai gurai) —
   5) Nan-kai ginkō kara okane o karita koto ga arimasu ka. (zenzen) —

6. Rei: kusuri o nomimasu — Kusuri o nonda hō ga ii desu.

   1) ashita kimasu —
   2) hayaku nemasu —
   3) koshō o naoshimasu —
   4) basu de ikimasu —
   5) ki o tsukemasu —
   6) erebētā o tsukaimasu —
   7) sensei ni kikimasu —
   8) tabako o yamemasu —
   9) Sentā ni imasu —
   10) hoteru ni tomarimasu —

7. Rei 1: Osoi desu kara, hayaku (ikimasu)
          —Osoi desu kara, hayaku itta hō ga ii desu.

   Rei 2: Ano mise wa takai desu kara, (kaimasen)
          —Ano mise wa takai desu kara, kawanai hō ga ii desu.

   1) Jikan ga arimasen kara, takushii ni (norimasu) —
   2) Ima Nihon-go o benkyō-shite imasu kara, Ei-go o (hanashimasen) —
   3) Kono kikai wa koshō-shite imasu kara, (tsukaimasen) —
   4) Abunai desu kara, kikai ni (sawarimasen) —
   5) Ano mise wa yasui desu kara, ano mise de (kaimasu) —
   6) Heya ga kurai desu kara, denki o (tsukemasu) —
   7) Samui desu kara, mado o (shimemasu) —
   8) Chikai desu kara, (arukimasu) —
   9) Karada ni warui desu kara, o-sake o (nomimasen) —
   10) Muzukashii desu kara, ano hito ni (kikimasu) —

8. Chāto 7

   1) Rei: Denwa o kaketa hō ga ii desu.
   2), 3), 4), 5), 6), 7), 8), 9)

9. Chāto 10

   1) Rei: Shinbun o yonda ato de, tegami o kakimasu.
   2), 3), 4), 5), 6), 7), 8), 9), 10)

Mondai

I. 1. Dōzo heya [   ] haitte kudasai.
   2. 1-ji ni uchi [   ] demashō.
   3. Watashi wa "doru" o "en" [   ] kaetai desu.
   4. Abebe-san wa isu [   ] suwatte imasu.
   5. Hayaku basu [   ] notte kudasai.
   6. Kikai [   ] sawaranai de kudasai.
   7. Tsugi no eki de densha [   ] orinakereba narimasen.
   8. Kinō Tanaka-san [   ] aimashita.
   9. Rao-san [   ] kiita hō ga ii desu.
   10. Kuni e kaette, sensei [   ] narimasu.

II. 1. Nihon no eiga o (miru—   ) koto ga arimasen.
                        (miru—   ) ni ikimashō.
                        (miru—   ) ato de, kaimono-shimasu.
   2. Rajio no koshō o (naosu—   ) koto ga dekimasu.
                        (naosu—   ) hō ga ii desu.
                        (naosu—   ) nakereba narimasen.
   3. Watashi no heya wa (akarui—   ) narimashita.
                          (akarui—   ), hiroi desu.
                          (akarui—   ) nai desu.

III. 1. Nihon de eiga o mita koto ga arimasu ka.
   2. Anata wa nan-kai hikōki ni notta koto ga arimasu ka.
   3. Nihon no o-sake o nonda koto ga arimasu ka.
   4. Anata wa Nihon-ryōri o tabeta koto ga arimasu ka.
   5. Jisshū no mae ni, nani o shimasu ka.
   6. Ōsaka kara Nagoya made jidōsha de itta hō ga ii desu ka, shinkansen de itta hō ga ii desu ka.
   7. Anata no kazoku wa Nihon e kita koto ga arimasu ka.
   8. Mainichi bangohan o tabeta ato de, nani o shimasu ka.
   9. Itsu kara ryokō ni ikimasu ka. ("—ato de" o tsukatte kudasai.)
   10. Nihon no umi de oyoida koto ga arimasu ka.

Dai 20 Ka

Bunkei

	Teinei-tai	Futsū-tai
Dōshi	kakimasu	kaku
	kakimasen	kakanai
	kakimashita	kaita
	kakimasendeshita	kakanakatta
(Reigai)		
	arimasu	aru
	arimasen	nai
	arimashita	atta
	arimasendeshita	nakatta
I-Keiyōshi	ōkii desu	ōkii
	ōkikunai desu	ōkikunai
	ōkikatta desu	ōkikatta
	ōkikunakatta desu	ōkikunakatta
Na-Keiyōshi Meishi	kirei desu	kirei da
	kirei dewa arimasen	kirei dewa nai
	kirei deshita	kirei datta
	kirei dewa arimasendeshita	kirei dewa nakatta

Kaiwa (5 ka no kaiwa no Futsū-tai)

Tanom: Genki?

Lee: Un, genki da yo.
Kimi wa dō?

Tanom: Boku mo genki da.
Kimi wa ashita doko e iku?

Lee: Doko mo ikanai yo.

Tanom: Jā, boku to issho ni Kyōto e ikanai?

Lee: Sore wa ii ne.

Reibun

1. Tanaka-san wa piano ga jōzu da.

2. Watashi wa kudamono ga suki da.

3. Watashi wa ima kamera ga hoshii.

4. Hayaku kuni e kaeritai.

5. Lee-san wa ima tabako o sutte iru.

6. Kono tēpu-rekōdā o tsukatte mo ii.

7. Watashi wa ii kamera o motte iru.

8. Watashi wa Rao-san no jūsho o shiranai.

9. Kenshūsei wa mainichi benkyō-shinakereba naranai.

10. Ima okane o harawanakute mo ii.

11. Jidōsha no unten ga dekiru.

12. Furansu-go o hanasu koto ga dekinai.

13. Watashi wa Fujisan o mita koto ga aru.

14. Watashi wa zenzen shinkansen ni notta koto ga nai.

15. Basu wa osoi kara, densha de itta hō ga ii.

Renshū A

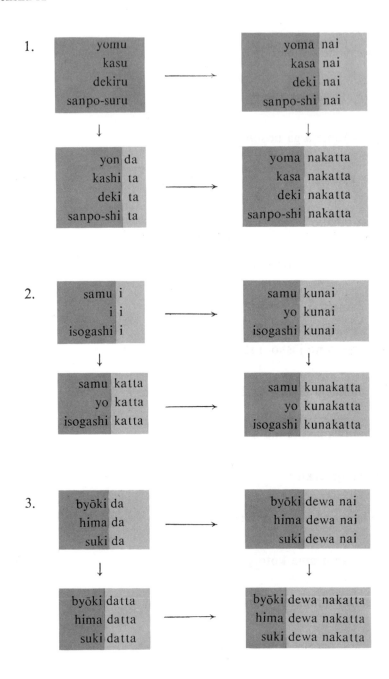

1.

yomu			yoma	nai
kasu			kasa	nai
dekiru			deki	nai
sanpo-suru			sanpo-shi	nai

↓ ↓

yon	da		yoma	nakatta
kashi	ta		kasa	nakatta
deki	ta		deki	nakatta
sanpo-shi	ta		sanpo-shi	nakatta

2.

samu	i		samu	kunai
i	i		yo	kunai
isogashi	i		isogashi	kunai

↓ ↓

samu	katta		samu	kunakatta
yo	katta		yo	kunakatta
isogashi	katta		isogashi	kunakatta

3.

byōki	da		byōki	dewa nai
hima	da		hima	dewa nai
suki	da		suki	dewa nai

↓ ↓

byōki	datta		byōki	dewa nakatta
hima	datta		hima	dewa nakatta
suki	datta		suki	dewa nakatta

Renshū B

1. 1) Rei: taberu — tabemasu
      tabenai —
      tabeta —
      tabenakatta —
   2) wakaru —
      wakaranai —
      wakatta —
      wakaranakatta —
   3) jisshū-suru —
      jisshū-shinai —
      jisshū-shita —
      jisshū-shinakatta —
   4) kuru —
      konai —
      kita —
      konakatta —
   5) atarashii —
      atarashikunai —
      atarashikatta —
      atarashikunakatta —
   6) ame da —
      ame dewa nai —
      ame datta —
      ame dewa nakatta —
   7) jōzu da —
      jōzu dewa nai —
      jōzu datta —
      jōzu dewa nakatta —
   8) hoshii —
      hoshikunai —
      hoshikatta —
      hoshikunakatta —

2. Rei: kaku — kakimasu
   1) nani mo tabenakatta —
   2) zenzen benkyō-shinai —
   3) niwa de shashin o totta —
   4) tabako o sutte iru —
   5) ano hito o shiranai —
   6) jikan ga nai —
   7) ashita shiken ga aru —
   8) tabako o sutte mo ii —
   9) mainichi benkyō-shinakereba naranai —
   10) Nihon-go o hanasu koto ga dekinai —
   11) Fujisan o mita koto ga aru —
   12) takushii de itta hō ga ii —
   13) amari atsukunai —
   14) ano hito wa kirei da —
   15) amari genki dewa nai —

3. Rei: nomimasu — nomu
   1) kōhii o nomimashita —
   2) tomodachi to terebi o mimasu —
   3) kōgi o kikimasu —
   4) tokei o shūri-shimasen —
   5) Nihon-go de hanashimasendeshita —
   6) tabako o suimasen —
   7) eki de Rao-san o machimasu —
   8) ima gohan o tabete imasu —
   9) okane o harawanakute mo ii desu —
   10) shinkansen ni notta koto ga arimasen —
   11) denwa o kaketa hō ga ii desu —
   12) kōjō de shashin o toru koto ga dekimasen —
   13) omoshiroi desu —
   14) karukute, ii desu —
   15) Kimura-san wa shinsetsu desu —
   16) kore wa chiisakute, yasui desu —
   17) amari shizuka dewa arimasen —
   18) kyō wa ii tenki dewa arimasen —
   19) watashi wa sakana ga suki desu —
   20) kinō wa kumori deshita —

4. Rei: Maiasa nan-ji ni okiru? (6-ji han)
      —6-ji han ni okimasu.
   1) Doko de asagohan o taberu? (Sentā no shokudō) —
   2) Nihon-go wa muzukashii? (iie, amari) —
   3) Gogo no benkyō wa nan-ji ni owaru? (5-ji) —
   4) Heya de donokurai benkyō-suru? (3-jikan gurai) —
   5) Donna supōtsu ga suki? (tenisu) —
   6) Kinō doko e itta? (Tōkyō) —
   7) Maiban nan-ji ni neru? (11-ji) —
   8) Donna kamera ga hoshii? (chiisai kamera) —
   9) Doko de sono kutsu o katta? (Yokohama) —
   10) Sukiyaki o tabeta koto ga aru? (iie) —

Mondai

I. [Nikki]　8-gatsu 22-nichi getsu-yōbi

Kesa 6-ji ni <u>okita</u>.　Onaka ga itakatta kara, nani mo tabenakatta.　Kaisha o
　　　Rei: okimashita
yasunde 11-ji made neta.　12-ji ni shokudō e itte gyūnyū o nonda.　Sorekara,

kusuri o kai ni itta.　300-en datta.　Kusuri o katta ato de, sugu Sentā e kaetta.

Neru mae ni kusuri o nonda.

II. [Anata no nikki]

Dai 21 Ka

Bunkei

1. Ashita Nihon-go no shiken ga aru to omoimasu.
2. Sensei wa "Jimusho e kite kudasai." to iimashita.
3. Ashita wa ame deshō. (. . . ame kamo shiremasen.)
4. Lee-san wa ashita kuru deshō. (. . . kuru kamo shiremasen.)

Kaiwa

Tanaka: Nihon ni tsuite dō omoimasu ka.

Lee: Sō desu ne. Kireina kuni da to omoimasu ga,
mada yoku wakarimasen.

Tanaka: Tanom-san wa Nihon wa mono ga takai to iimashita.

Lee: Watashi mo sō omoimasu.

Tanaka: Tokuni, tabemono ga takai deshō.

Lee: Sō desu ne.
Shikashi, denki-seihin wa watashi no kuni yori zutto yasui desu.

Tanaka: Jā, katte kaerimasu ka.

Lee: Ē, sō shitai desu.

Reibun

1. Nihon-jin o dō omoimasu ka.
   —Shinsetsu da to omoimasu.
   —Amari shinsetsu dewa nai to omoimasu.

2. Kono shiken wa dō desu ka.
   —Muzukashii to omoimasu.
   —Amari muzukashikunai to omoimasu.

3. Kesa no shiken wa dō deshita ka.
   —Hijōni muzukashikatta to omoimasu.
   —Sonnani muzukashikunakatta to omoimasu.

4. Tanom-san wa ashita kimasu ka.
   —Hai, kuru to omoimasu.
   —Iie, konai to omoimasu.

5. Kinō pātii ga arimashita ka.
   —Hai, atta to omoimasu.
   —Iie, nakatta to omoimasu.

6. Sensei wa nan to iimashita ka.
   —Kaette mo ii to iimashita.

7. Ano hito wa Nihon-go o hanasu koto ga dekimasu ka.
   —Tabun dekiru deshō.

8. Nihon-go wa omoshiroi deshō.
   —Ē, omoshiroi desu.

Renshū A

1. Ali-san wa

| uchi ni iru |
| okane ga nai |
| Tōkyō e itta |
| koko e konakatta |
| - - - - - - - - - |
| atama ga ii |
| amari omokunai |
| - - - - - - - - - |
| kenshūsei da |
| Tai-jin dewa nai |
| - - - - - - - - - |
| uta ga jōzu da |
| genki dewa nai |

to omoimasu.

2. Tanom-san wa

| "Kyōshitsu e ikimashō." |
| "Ohayō gozaimasu." |

to iimashita.

3. Rao-san wa

| ashita shiken ga aru |
| Tōkyō e ikanai |
| - - - - - - - - - - - - - - - |
| kono hon wa taihen omoshiroi |
| kono ryōri wa oishikunai |
| - - - - - - - - - - - - - - - |
| ashita wa yasumi da |
| kore wa sensei no dewa nai |
| - - - - - - - - - - - - - - - |
| taihen genki da |
| Nihon-jin wa shinsetsu dewa nai |

to iimashita.

4.

| Arora-san wa ashita kuni e kaeru |
| Tanom-san wa koko e konai |
| - - - - - - - - - - - - - - - |
| Ano eiga wa omoshiroi |
| Kono shiken wa muzukashikunai |
| - - - - - - - - - - - - - - - |
| Cortez-san wa byōki |
| Kore wa Tanom-san no hon dewa nai |
| - - - - - - - - - - - - - - - |
| Rao-san wa niku ga kirai |
| Ashita wa hima dewa nai |

deshō.
kamo shiremasen.

Renshū B

1. Rei 1: Arora-san wa shinsetsu desu
   —Arora-san wa shinsetsu da to omoimasu.
   Rei 2: ashita ame ga furimasu
   —Ashita ame ga furu to omoimasu.
   1) Arora-san wa omoshiroi hito desu —
   2) Arora-san wa uta ga jōzu desu —
   3) Arora-san wa atama ga ii desu —
   4) Cortez-san wa okane ga arimasen —
   5) Cortez-san wa kekkon-shite imasu —
   6) Cortez-san wa kinō Kyōto e ikimashita —

2. Rei: Nihon wa tabemono ga takai desu ka. (iie)
   —Iie, takakunai to omoimasu.
   1) Nihon wa atsui desu ka. (iie) —
   2) Abebe-san wa Nihon-go ga jōzu desu ka. (hai) —
   3) Ali-san wa Nihon-ryōri ga suki desu ka. (iie) —
   4) Konban ame ga furimasu ka. (iie) —
   5) Lee-san wa kodomo ga arimasu ka. (hai) —
   6) Lee-san wa jidōsha o motte imasu ka. (iie) —

3. Rei: kinō wa samukatta desu
   —Tanom-san wa <u>kinō wa samukatta</u> to iimashita.
   1) ashita shiken ga arimasu —
   2) Nihon no tabemono ga suki desu —
   3) ryokō wa tanoshikatta desu —
   4) kinō no ban pātii ga arimashita —
   5) jidōsha no unten ga dekimasen —
   6) hayaku kuni e kaeritai desu —
   7) minasan ni yoroshiku —

4. Rei: Lee-san wa Nihon-go o hanashimasu ka.
   —Tabun <u>hanasu</u> deshō.
   1) Slamet-san wa tabako o suimasu ka. —
   2) Rao-san wa niku o tabemasu ka. —
   3) Ali-san wa ashita isogashii desu ka. —
   4) Cortez-san wa kuni e kaerimashita ka. —
   5) Ashita wa ame desu ka. —
   6) Arora-san wa rainen kekkon-shimasu ka. —

5. Rei: ano hito wa sake ga suki desu
   —Ano hito wa sake ga suki kamo shiremasen.

   1) ashita shiken ga arimasu —
   2) ashita wa hima desu —
   3) kanai ga Nihon e kimasu —
   4) ashita wa ame desu —
   5) ashita kōjō e ikimasu —
   6) Cortez-san wa kuni e kaerimasu —

6. Rei: Nihon wa mono ga takai deshō.
      —Ē, takai desu.

   1) Nihon wa samui deshō. —
   2) Kinō wa samukatta deshō. —
   3) Anata wa dokushin deshō. —
   4) Kinō Tōkyō wa ame datta deshō. —
   5) Anata wa Katō-san o shiranai deshō. —
   6) Anata wa sukiyaki o tabeta koto ga nai deshō. —

7. Rei: Asa sensei ya tomodachi ni aimasu. Nan to iimasu ka.
      —"Ohayō gozaimasu." to iimasu.

   1) Ban tomodachi ni aimasu. Nan to iimasu ka.
   2) Gohan o taberu mae ni, Nihon-jin wa nan to iimasu ka.
   3) Gohan o tabeta ato de, Nihon-jin wa nan to iimasu ka.
   4) Tomodachi ga kuni e kaerimasu. Nan to iimasu ka.
   5) Tomodachi ga "Arigatō." to iimashita.
      Anata wa nan to iimasu ka.

Mondai

I. Rei: Nihon-ryōri wa oishii desu ka.
         —Hai, Nihon-ryōri wa oishii to omoimasu.

  1. Anata no kazoku wa o-genki desu ka.
     —Hai,

  2. Kaisha no hito wa ashita kimasu ka.
     —Iie,

  3. Ashita shiken ga arimasu ka.
     —Iie,

  4. Nihon-go de hanasanakereba narimasen ka.
     —Hai,

  5. Nihon-go wa muzukashii desu ka.
     —Iie,

  6. Garcia-san wa mō byōin e ikimashita ka.
     —Hai,

II.

Ashita {
Rei: ii tenki desu—ii tenki
1. Nihon-go no shiken ga arimasu—
2. kōjō-kengaku wa omoshiroi desu—
3. tomodachi ga kimasu—
} deshō.

Ano hito wa {
4. Indo-jin desu—
5. kekkon-shite imasu—
6. Nihon-go ga mada wakarimasen—
7. niku o zenzen tabemasen—
} kamo shiremasen.

III. 1. Nihon-jin wa gohan o taberu mae ni, nan to iimasu ka.

    2. Nihon o dō omoimasu ka.

    3. Kazoku no minasan wa o-genki desu ka.

    4. Nihon no kudamono wa takai to omoimasu ka.

    5. Ashita ame ga furu to omoimasu ka.

Dai 22 Ka

Bunkei

1. Heya o deru toki, denki o keshite kudasai.
2. Ame no toki, uchi ni imasu.
3. Okane ga nai to, komarimasu.
4. Migi e magaru to, depāto ga arimasu.

Kaiwa

Tanaka: Anata wa kōjō e iku toki, itsumo dōyatte ikimasu ka.

Ali: Komagome de densha ni notte, Shinagawa de norikaemasu. Soshite, Kawasaki de orimasu.

Tanaka: Watashi wa ashita anata no kōjō e ikitai desu ga, michi o oshiete kudasai.

Ali: Eki kara massugu 100-mētoru gurai aruku to, kōsaten ga arimasu.

Tanaka: Kōsaten desu ne. Soko o watarimasu ka.

Ali: Iie, hidari e magatte kudasai.
50-mētoru iku to, hashi ga arimasu.
Hashi o wataru to, migi ni kōjō ga arimasu.

Tanaka: Arigatō, yoku wakarimashita.

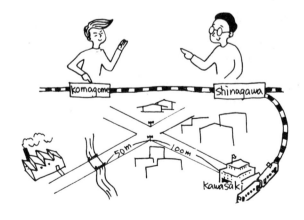

Reibun

1. Isogashii toki, tetsudatte kudasai.

2. Himana toki, asobi ni kite kudasai.

3. Michi o aruku toki, jidōsha ni chūi-shimashō.

4. Tōkyō e itta toki, kono kutsu o kaimashita.

5. Kodomo no toki, doko ni sunde imashita ka.
   —Ōsaka ni sunde imashita.

6. Okane ga nai toki, dō shimasu ka.
   —Tomodachi kara karimasu.

7. Tomodachi ga kekkon-suru toki, nan to iimasu ka.
   —"Omedetō gozaimasu." to iimasu.

8. Kaimono-suru toki ya ryokō-suru toki, pasupōto ga irimasu.

9. O-sake o nomu to, tanoshiku narimasu.

10. Motto benkyō-shinai to, komarimasu yo.

Renshū A

1.

Gohan o taberu	toki,	hashi o tsukaimasu.
Tōkyō e iku		densha ni norimasu.
Jikan ga nai		takushii de ikimasu.
Imi ga wakaranai		jisho o mite kudasai.
Hiroshima e itta		o-miyage o kaimashita.
Arora-san o mita		kirei da to omoimashita.

2.

Samu i	toki,	ōbā o kimasu.
Nemu i		atsui kōhii o nonde kudasai.
Hima na		hon o yomimasu.
Shizuka na		yoku neru koto ga dekimashita.
Ame no		soto e demasen.
Kodomo no		Manira ni sunde imashita.

3.

Satō o ireru	to,	amaku narimasu.
Hidari e magaru		migi ni eki ga arimasu.
Gohan o tabenai		byōki ni narimasu.
Okane ga nai		nani mo kau koto ga dekimasen.

Renshū B

1. 1) Rei: Ryokō no toki, <u>pasupōto</u> o motte itte kudasai.
   (sētā, pen to nōto, chiisai kaban, okane, kasa)
   2) Rei: Himana toki, <u>terebi o mimasu.</u>
   (tegami o kakimasu, hon o yomimasu, rekōdo o kikimasu,
   tomodachi ni denwa o kakemasu, ryokō-shimasu)
   3) Rei: <u>Atsui</u> toki, dō shimasu ka.
   (isogashii, okane ga hoshii, okane ga nai, biiru o nomitai,
   denwa o kaketai, sabishii, nemui)

2. Rei: <u>Gohan o taberu</u> toki, doko e ikimasu ka.
   1) (terebi o mimasu)   4) (pinpon-shimasu)
   2) (Nihon-go o benkyō-shimasu)   5) (tomodachi to hanashimasu)
   3) (kitte o kaimasu)   6) (denwa o kakemasu)

3. Rei: heya o demasu, denki o keshimasu
   —Heya o deru toki, denki o keshimasu.
   1) okane ga arimasen, tomodachi kara karimasu —
   2) jidōsha o shūri-shimasu, supana o tsukaimasu —
   3) wakarimasen, sensei ni kikimasu —
   4) michi o arukimasu, jidōsha ni chūi-shimashō —
   5) Tōkyō e ikimashita, kono kamera o kaimashita —

4. 1) Rei: <u>Okane</u> ga nai to, komarimasu.
   (uchi, kasa, pasupōto, jisho, tokei)
   2) Rei: Migi e magaru to, <u>hana-ya</u> ga arimasu.
   (kōsaten, hashi, gakkō, eki, kōjō, depāto)

5. Rei: <u>Ame ga furu</u> to, komarimasu.
   1) (takushii ga kimasen)   4) (pasupōto o nakushimasu)
   2) (kasa ga arimasen)   5) (Nihon-go ga dekimasen)
   3) (shiken ga arimasu)   6) (byōki ni narimasu)

6. Rei: kusuri o nomimasu, kaze ga naorimasu
   —Kusuri o nomu to, kaze ga naorimasu.
   1) massugu ikimasu, kōsaten ga arimasu —
   2) mizu ga arimasen, komarimasu —
   3) yoru ni narimasu, samuku narimasu —
   4) takushii de ikimasu, 1-jikan kakarimasu —
   5) tabako o yamemasu, karada ni ii desu —

7. Michi o oshiemashō.
   Rei: Kōjō e iku toki, dōyatte ikimasu ka.
        —Eki kara massugu 100-mētoru gurai aruku to, kōsaten ga arimasu.
        Soko o hidari e magatte kudasai. 50-mētoru aruku to, hashi ga arimasu.
        Hashi o wataru to, migi ni kōjō ga arimasu.
   1) Yūbinkyoku e iku toki, dōyatte ikimasu ka.
   2) Tanaka-san no uchi e dōyatte ikimasu ka.
   3) Byōin e dōyatte ikimasu ka.

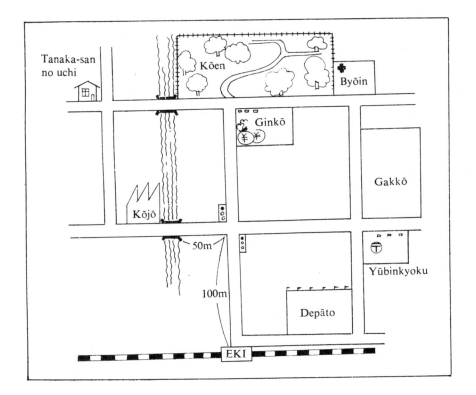

Mondai

I. Rei: Gohan o (tabemasu—taberu) toki, shokudō e ikimasu.
   1. Watashi wa (hima desu—   ) toki, kaimono ni ikimasu.
   2. Tomodachi ga (kekkon-shimasu—   ) toki, "Omedetō gozaimasu."
      to iimasu.
   3. Nihon-go ga (wakarimasen—   ) to, kōjō de komarimasu.
   4. Anata wa (sabishii desu—   ) toki, dō shimasu ka.
   5. Nihon e (tsukimashita—   ) toki, ame ga futte imashita.
   6. Tegami ga (kimasen—   ) to, sabishii desu.

II. Rei: Ame no toki, _____ eki made takushii de ikimasu. _____
   1. Atama ga itai toki, _____ .
   2. Denki o kesu to, _____ .
   3. _____ toki, okane ga irimasu.
   4. _____ to, nemuku narimasu.
   5. _____ toki, sensei ni kikimasu.

III. 1. Samui toki, dō shimasu ka.
    2. Okane ga nai toki, dō shimasu ka.
    3. Sentā o deru toki, uketsuke no hito ni nan to iimasu ka.
    4. Byōki no toki, doko e itte kusuri o moraimasu ka.
    5. Anata wa himana toki, nani o shimasu ka.

Dai 23 Ka

Bunkei

1. Kinō kita hito wa Kimura-san no tomodachi desu.
2. Kore wa watashi ga totta shashin desu.
3. Senshū anata ga katta kamera o misete kudasai.
4. Tegami o kaku jikan ga arimasen.

Kaiwa

Tanaka: Kenshū-ryokō ni tsuite shitsumon ga arimasu ka.

Slamet: Nagoya de kengaku-suru kōjō wa donna kōjō desu ka.

Tanaka: Jidōsha o tsukutte iru kōjō de, Nihon de ichiban
ōkina mēkā desu.

Slamet: Nagoya no tsugi ni iku tokoro wa doko desu ka.

Tanaka: Hiroshima desu.
Koko de Heiwa-kōen to kikai no kōjō o mimasu.

Slamet: Hiroshima ni watashi no tomodachi ga imasu ga,
kare ni au jikan ga arimasu ka.

Tanaka: Sā, amari nai to omoimasu yo.
Hoka ni shitsumon wa.

Slamet: Arimasen.

Reibun

1. Kinō Sentā e kita hito wa dare desu ka.
   —Watashi no kaisha no hito desu.

2. Asoko de uta o utatte iru hito wa dare desu ka.
   —Tanom-san desu.

3. Anata ga sukina supōtsu wa nan desu ka.
   —Futtobōru desu.

4. Kinō watashi ga mita eiga wa omoshirokatta desu.

5. Kore wa dare ga totta shashin desu ka.
   —Tanaka-san ga totta shashin desu.
   Doko de totta shashin desu ka.
   —Kyōto de totta shashin desu.
   Itsu totta shashin desu ka.
   —Senshū no nichi-yōbi ni totta shashin desu.

6. Jisho o utte iru tokoro o shitte imasu ka.
   —Hai, shitte imasu.

7. Ima made kiita kōgi no naka de nani ga ichiban
   omoshirokatta desu ka.

Renshū A

1. Ashita koko e kuru | hito | wa Tanaka-san desu.
   Ashita koko e konai
   Kinō koko e kita
   Kinō koko e konakatta

2. Are wa | konban watashi ga yomu | hon | desu.
   kinō watashi ga katta
   watashi ga hoshii
   watashi ga yomitai
   Arora-san ga sukina

3. Raishū kengaku-suru | tokoro | o shitte imasu ka.
   Kippu o kau
   Rao-san ga sunde iru
   Jisho o utte iru
   Garcia-san ga hataraite iru

4. Tegami o kaku | jikan | ga arimasen.
   Rekōdo o kiku
   Terebi o miru
   Hon o yomu
   Nihon-go o benkyō-suru

Renshū B

1. Chāto 3

   1) Rei: Kore wa watashi ga katta <u>hon</u> desu.

                                           4) (matchi)

   2) (enpitsu)   5) (rajio)

   3) (kaban)   6) (terebi)

2. Chāto 3

   7) Rei: Sore wa doko de katta <u>zasshi</u> desu ka.

                                       10) (kamera)

   8) (tokei)   11) (tabako)

   9) (shinbun)   12) (jidōsha)

3. Rei: <u>Supein-go o hanasu</u> hito wa dare desu ka.

   1) (terebi no shūri ga dekimasu)

   2) (kinō Sentā e kimashita)

   3) (kodomo ga arimasu)

   4) (mada kekkon-shite imasen)

   5) (okane ga zenzen arimasen)

   6) (Ginza e itta koto ga arimasu)

4. Chāto 5

   1) Rei: Asoko de <u>gohan o tabete iru</u> hito wa dare desu ka.

   2) (hana o kau)

   3) (tabako o suu)

   4) (kōhii o nomu)

   5) (shashin o toru)

   6) (rekōdo o kiku)

   7) (hon o yomu)

   8) (tegami o kaku)

   9) (terebi o miru)

   10) (Nihon-go o benkyō-suru)

5. Rei: (anata wa kaimashita) kamera wa dore desu ka
    —Anata ga katta kamera wa dore desu ka.
    1) (anata wa ikimasu) kōjō wa doko desu ka —
    2) (anata wa suki desu) nomimono wa nan desu ka —
    3) (anata wa umaremashita) tokoro wa doko desu ka —
    4) (anata wa norimashita) hikōki wa nan desu ka —
    5) (anata wa hon o kaimashita) depāto wa doko desu ka —
    6) (anata wa Rao-san ni kashimashita) hon wa dore desu ka —
    7) (anata wa ima motte imasu) kamera o misete kudasai —
    8) (anata wa ima sunde imasu) tokoro o oshiete kudasai —

6. Chāto 3

    1) Rei: (Tōkyō de kaimashita)
            —Kore wa Tōkyō de katta hon desu.
    2) (Tanaka-san kara moraimashita) —
    3) (Cortez-san kara karimashita) —
    4) (Rao-san ga kaimashita) —
    5) (Slamet-san ga shūri-shimashita) —
    6) (ano kōjō de tsukutte imasu) —
    7) (Nihon ni arimasen) —
    8) (Honkon de kaimashita) —
    9) (Burajiru-jin ga yomimasu) —
    10) (tsukai-kata ga kantan desu) —
    11) (Iran kara motte kimashita) —
    12) (watashi ga kaitai desu) —

7. Rei: Anata ga ikitai kuni wa doko desu ka. (Mekishiko)
        —Mekishiko desu.
    1) Pinpon ga jōzuna hito wa dare desu ka. (Tanom-san) —
    2) Kimura-san ga katta o-miyage wa dore desu ka. (kore) —
    3) Jimusho de hataraite iru hito wa nan-nin desu ka. (daitai 50-nin) —
    4) Konoaida mita eiga wa dō deshita ka. (taihen omoshirokatta) —
    5) Sore wa dare kara karita hon desu ka. (tomodachi) —
    6) Kore wa itsu totta shashin desu ka. (sengetsu) —

Mondai

I. Rei: Kinō Sentā e kita hito wa (dare) desu ka.

1. Anata ga sukina kudamono wa (   ) desu ka.
2. Rao-san ga jisshū-suru kōjō wa (   ) desu ka.
3. Sore wa (   ) de katta tokei desu ka.
4. Robii de shinbun o yonde iru kenshūsei wa (   ) desu ka.
5. Kore wa (   ) ga totta shashin desu ka.
6. Nichi-yōbi ni anata ga mita eiga wa (   ) deshita ka.
7. Denki-seihin o utte iru tokoro wa (   ) desu ka.
8. Ima made kiita kōgi no naka de (   ) ga ichiban omoshirokatta desu ka.

II.
1. Anata ga jisshū-suru kōjō wa doko ni arimasu ka.
2. Senshū kengaku-shita kōjō wa doko desu ka.
3. Kurasu no naka de kekkon-shite iru hito wa dare desu ka.
4. Anata ni Nihon-go o oshiete iru sensei wa dare desu ka.
5. Anata ga issho ni benkyō-shite iru kenshūsei wa doko no kuni no hito desu ka.
6. Anata ga sukina supōtsu wa nan desu ka.
7. Anata ga kiraina tabemono wa nan desu ka.
8. Ima made kengaku-shita kōjō no naka de doko ga yokatta desu ka.
9. Nihon de anata ga kaitai mono wa nan desu ka.
10. Anata wa ima jidōsha o kau okane ga arimasu ka.

Dai 24 Ka

Bunkei

1. Nihon-go o hanasu koto wa muzukashii desu.
2. Watashi no shumi wa e o kaku koto desu.
3. Watashi wa jazu o kiku koto ga suki desu.
4. [Anata wa] ano hito ga kaetta koto o shitte imasu ka.

Kaiwa

Kimura: Anata wa donokurai Nihon-go o benkyō-shimashita ka.
Rao: 4-shūkan desu.
Kimura: Hontō desu ka. Jōzu desu ne.
Nihon-go o hanasu koto wa muzukashii desu ka.
Rao: Ē, muzukashii desu.
Kimura: Hiragana ya katakana o yomu koto ga dekimasu ka.
Rao: Iie, mada desu.
Ima rōmaji de benkyō-shite imasu.
Korekara, kaku koto o naraitai desu.
Kimura: Sō desu ka.
Ganbatte kudasai.

Reibun

1. Tabako o suu koto wa karada ni warui desu.

2. Anata no shumi wa nan desu ka.
   —Ongaku o kiku koto ya gitā o hiku koto nado desu.

3. Anata wa donna supōtsu ga suki desu ka.
   —Yakyū desu.
   Jibun de shimasu ka.
   —Iie, miru koto ga suki desu.

4. [Anata wa] ashita shiken ga nai koto o shitte imasu ka.
   —Iie, shirimasen.

5. [Anata wa] raishū Rao-san no okusan ga kuru koto o kikimashita ka.
   —Hai, kikimashita.

Renshū A

1.

Nihon-go o hanasu Maiasa sanpo-suru Tabako o suu Tomodachi ga nai	koto	wa	muzukashii desu. karada ni ii desu. yokunai desu. sabishii desu.

2.

Watashi no shumi wa

ongaku o kiku gitā o hiku hon o yomu hitori de ryokō-suru	koto	desu.

3.

Watashi wa

benkyō-suru oyogu terebi o miru uta o utau	koto	ga suki desu.

4.

Ashita Tanaka-san ga kuru Ano hito ga kuni e kaetta Ashita shiken ga nai Ali-san ga Ōsaka ni sunde iru	koto	o shitte imasu ka.

Renshū B

1. Rei: <u>Nihon-go o hanasu</u> koto **wa** muzukashii desu.
   1) (Nihon-go o kikimasu)
   2) (jidōsha o unten-shimasu)
   3) (hashi de tabemasu)
   4) (kanji de kakimasu)
   5) (Nihon-go de setsumei-shimasu)
   6) (tabako o yamemasu)

2. Rei: Watashi no shumi wa **piano o hiku** koto desu.
   1) (e o kakimasu)
   2) (ongaku o kikimasu)
   3) (eiga o mimasu)
   4) (uta o utaimasu)
   5) (shashin o torimasu)
   6) (gitā o hikimasu)

3. Rei: uta o utaimasu, Arora-san wa jōzu desu
      —Arora-san wa <u>uta o utau</u> koto ga jōzu desu.
   1) oyogimasu, Lee-san wa jōzu desu —
   2) ryōri o tsukurimasu, Kimura-san wa jōzu desu —
   3) rajio o kumitatemasu, watashi wa suki desu —
   4) hatarakimasu, watashi wa suki desu —
   5) yama o arukimasu, watashi no koibito wa suki desu —
   6) Nihon-go o benkyō-shimasu, ano hito wa kirai desu —

4. Rei: Rao-san wa ikimasu, shitte imasu ka
      —<u>Rao-san ga iku</u> koto o shitte imasu ka.
   1) Rao-san wa ashita kimasu, kikimashita ka —
   2) Rao-san wa raigetsu kekkon-shimasu, shitte imasu —
   3) Tanom-san wa Sentā ni sunde imasu, kikimashita —
   4) kyō shiken ga arimasu, wasuremashita —
   5) Garcia-san wa Supein-go o hanashimasu, shirimasendeshita —
   6) uketsuke de okane o harawanakereba narimasen, shitte imasu ka —

Mondai

I. Rei: Hashi de taberu koto [wa] muzukashii desu.
1. Tomodachi ni au koto [   ] taihen tanoshii desu.
2. Nihon-go de hanasu koto [   ] omoshiroi desu.
3. Jidōsha no koshō o naosu koto [   ] dekimasu.
4. Gitā o hiku koto [   ] sonnani yasashikunai desu.
5. Ashita shiken ga aru koto [   ] shitte imasu ka.
6. Hitori de Kyūshū e iku koto [   ] dekimasen.
7. Tanom-san ga kuni e kaetta koto [   ] kikimashita.
8. Tomodachi to issho ni o-sake o nomu koto [   ] suki desu.
9. Hanasu koto [   ] kiku koto [   ], dochira ga muzukashii desu ka.
10. Nihon-go o narau koto [   ] dō omoimasu ka.

II. 1. Anata no shumi wa nan desu ka.
2. Nihon e kuru mae ni, 5-shūkan Nihon-go o benkyō-suru koto o shitte imashita ka.
3. Anata wa Ei-go o hanasu koto ga dekimasu ka.
4. Nihon no uta o utau koto ga dekimasu ka.
5. Do-yōbi no gogo benkyō ga nai koto o shitte imasu ka.
6. Benkyō-suru koto to, asobu koto to, dochira ga omoshiroi desu ka.
7. Rajio o kumitateru koto to, bunkai suru koto to, dochira ga yasashii desu ka.
8. Nihon-go o hanasu koto wa muzukashii to omoimasu ka.
9. Anata wa shashin o toru koto ga jōzu desu ka.
10. Anata wa eiga o miru koto ga suki desu ka.

Fukushū A

I. (   ) no naka ni joshi 'e', 'de' matawa 'ni' o irete kudasai.

1. Nihon (   ) jisshū-shimasu.
2. Nihon (   ) jisshū ni kimashita.
3. Koko (   ) hon ga arimasu.
4. Koko (   ) tabako o sutte mo ii desu.
5. Kinō Ginza (   ) ikimashita.
6. Ginza (   ) kaimono-shimashita.
7. Kanai wa kuni (   ) imasu.
8. Ashita kuni (   ) kaerimasu.
9. Ima Kenshū Sentā (   ) sunde imasu.
10. Kenshū Sentā (   ) Nihon-go o benkyō-shimashita.

II. (   ) no naka ni joshi 'ga' matawa 'o' o irete kudasai.

1. Watashi wa kōhii (   ) suki desu.
2. Atsui kōhii (   ) nomimashita.
3. Depāto de terebi (   ) kaimashita.
4. Watashi wa terebi (   ) hoshii desu.
5. Koko ni terebi (   ) arimasu.
6. Watashi wa Nihon-go (   ) benkyō-shitai desu.
7. Anata wa Nihon-go (   ) wakarimasu ka.
8. Watashi wa Nihon-go (   ) heta desu.
9. Ano hito wa ii jisho (   ) motte imasu.
10. Watashi wa ima okane (   ) arimasen.

III. (   ) no naka ni joshi o irete kudasai.

1. Watashi wa tomodachi (   ) tokei (   ) moraimashita.
2. Byōki desu (   ), ashita kaisha (   ) yasumimasu.
3. Gohan (   ) pan (   ), dochira (   ) suki desu ka.
4. Sore wa doko (   ) kamera desu ka.
5. Watashi wa onaka (   ) itai desu.
6. Kinō doko (   ) ikimasendeshita.
7. Kinō no ban dare (   ) kimashita ka.
8. Nihon e terebi (   ) benkyō (   ) kimashita.
9. Kuni e kaette kara, sensei (   ) narimasu.
10. Taipu (   ) tsukai-kata (   ) shitte imasu.

Dai 25 Ka

Bunkei

1. Yukkuri hanashitara, wakarimasu.
2. Wakaranakattara, watashi ni kiite kudasai.
3. Okane ga attara, Indo e ikitai desu.
4. Ame ga futte mo, ikimasu.
5. Ikura shirabete mo, wakarimasen.

Kaiwa

Lee: Dōyatte kono kikai o tsukaimasu ka.

Katō: Hajime ni suitchi o irete, tsugi ni kono botan o osu to, ugokimasu.

Lee: Kantan desu ne.

Katō: Ē, shikashi akai ranpu ga tsuitara, koshō desu kara, sugu tomete kudasai.

Lee: Koshō no toki, dō shitara ii desu ka.

Katō: Tesutā o tsukatte, yoku shirabete kudasai.

Soredemo wakaranakattara, watashi o yobi ni kite kudasai.

Reibun

1. Yokohama e ittara, dare ni aitai desu ka.
   —Slamet-san ni aitai desu.

2. Moshi ashita ame dattara, dō shimasu ka.
   —Ichinichi-jū uchi ni imasu.

3. Nichi-yōbi watashi to issho ni ikimasen ka.
   —Hima dattara ikimasu ga, isogashikattara ikimasen.

4. Doko de okane o kaetara ii desu ka.
   —Ano ginkō de kaetara ii desu.

5. Ginkō wa dō ittara ii desu ka.
   —Kono michi o massugu itte kudasai.

6. Hon o karitai desu ga, dō shitara ii desu ka.
   —Uketsuke no hito ni kiite kudasai.

7. Yasukattara, kaimasu ka.
   —Hai, yasukattara, kaimasu.
   —Iie, yasukute mo, kaimasen.

8. Ame ga futte mo, ikimasu ka.
   —Hai, ame ga futte mo, ikimasu.
   —Iie, ame ga futtara, ikimasen.

Renshū A

1.

kau	kattara		kawanai	kawanakattara
iku			ikanai	
yomu			yomanai	
yasumu			yasumanai	
aru			nai	
owaru			owaranai	
wakaru			wakaranai	
komaru			komaranai	
au			awanai	
tsukareru			tsukawanai	
wasureru			wasurenai	
kuru			konai	
suru			shinai	

2. 1)

Yukkuri hanashita	ra	wakarimasu.
Ame ga futta	ra	ikimasen.
Wakaranakatta	ra	watashi ni kiite kudasai.
Yasukatta	ra	kaimasu.
Hima datta	ra	asobi ni kite kudasai.

2)

Doko de katta	ra	ii desu ka.
Dare ni kiita	ra	
Itsu itta	ra	

3)

Ame ga futte	mo	ikimasu.
Kuni e kaette	mo	wasuremasen.
Takakute	mo	kaimasu.
Ame de	mo	ikimasu.
Hitori de	mo	ikimasu.

4)

Ikura	benkyō-shite	mo	oboemasen.
	shirabete	mo	wakarimasen.
	matte	mo	kimasen.

Renshū B

1. Rei: Anata ga <u>ittara</u>, watashi mo <u>ikimasu</u>.

1)	(ikanai)	4)	(kaeru)
2)	(kau)	5)	(kaeranai)
3)	(kawanai)	6)	(utau)
		7)	(utawanai)

2. Rei: yasui, kaimasu — Yasukattara, kaimasu.
   1) ii, kaimasu —
   2) warui, kaimasen —
   3) isogashii, ikimasen —
   4) omoshiroi, mimasu —
   5) osoi, takushii de ikimasu —

3. Rei: ame, ikimasen — Ame dattara, ikimasen.
   1) ii tenki, ikimasu —
   2) Nihon-go, wakarimasu —
   3) hima, asobi ni kite kudasai —
   4) byōki, kaisha o yasumimasu —
   5) ashita, ikimasu —

4. Rei: <u>Okane ga nakattara</u>, dō shimasu ka.
   1) (Nihon-jin ga issho ni ikimasen)
   2) (Nihon-go ga wakarimasen)
   3) (Tanom-san ga kimasen)
   4) (9-ji no densha ni noru koto ga dekimasen)
   5) (jikan ga arimasen)

5. Rei: Tōkyō e ikimasu, watashi no tomodachi ni aimasu
   　　—Tōkyō e <u>ittara</u>, watashi no tomodachi ni <u>atte kudasai</u>.
   1) jikan ga arimasu, tegami o kakimasu —
   2) basu ga arimasen, arukimasu —
   3) tsukaremasu, sukoshi yasumimasu —

4) hon o karimasu, ato de kaeshimasu —

5) genki ni narimasu, mata kimasu —

6) wakarimasen, shitsumon-shimasu —

6. Rei: Doko de okane o kaemasu ka.
—Doko de okane o kaetara ii desu ka.

1) Doko de jisho o kaimasu ka. —

2) Dare ni kikimasu ka. —

3) Koshō no toki, dō shimasu ka. —

4) Doko ni denwa o kakemasu ka. —

5) Itsu anata no uchi e ikimasu ka. —

6) Kyō nani o shimasu ka. —

7. Rei: Ikura benkyō-shite mo, wakarimasen.

1) (yomu)   4) (shiraberu)

2) (kiku)   5) (narau)

3) (kangaeru)   6) (hanasu)

8. Rei 1: yasui, kaimasen — Yasukute mo, kaimasen.
Rei 2: ame, ikimasu — Ame demo, ikimasu.

1) takai, kaimasu —

2) hima, tetsudaimasen —

3) kirai, tabemasu —

4) yasumi, hatarakimasu —

5) tōi, aruite ikimasu —

6) kotoba wa onaji desu, kuni wa chigaimasu —

9. Rei: ame ga furimasu, ikimasu — Ame ga futte mo, ikimasu.

1) ima oboemasu, sugu wasuremasu —

2) okane o karimasu, zenzen kaeshimasen —

3) byōki ni narimasu, sake o yamemasen —

4) ikura yobimasu, kimasen —

5) ikura shūri-shimasu, yoku narimasen —

6) ikura oshimasu, ugokimasen —

Mondai

I. Rei: Yukkuri hanashitara, _____ wakarimasu. _____

    1. Takushii ga konakattara, _____.

    2. _____ ra, watashi no uchi e kite kudasai.

    3. Minasan ni attara, _____.

    4. Kuni kara tegami ga kitara, _____.

    5. Dare ni kiite mo, _____.

II. Rei: (Nani) o tabetara ii desu ka.

    1. (_____) de okane o kaetara ii desu ka.

    2. Wakaranai toki, (_____) ni kiitara ii desu ka.

    3. Ryokō ni (_____) o motte ittara ii desu ka.

    4. (_____)-ji ni denwa o kaketara ii desu ka.

    5. Koshō no toki, (_____) shitara ii desu ka.

III. 1. Nichi-yōbi ni ii o-tenki dattara, doko e ikimasu ka.

    2. Maiasa nan-ji ni kyōshitsu e kitara ii desu ka.

    3. Tsukaretara, dō shimasu ka.

    4. Okane ga nakattara, dō shimasu ka.

    5. Nan de Tōkyō e ittara, ichiban hayai desu ka.

    6. Moshi 100-man-en attara, nani o kaimasu ka.

    7. Onaka ga itai toki, dō shitara ii desu ka.

    8 Maiban donokurai benkyō-shitara, Nihon-go ga jōzu ni narimasu ka.

    9. Ame ga futte mo, kaisha e ikimasu ka.

    10. Sukoshi atama ga itakute mo, benkyō-shimasu ka.

Dai 26 Ka

Bunkei

1. Watashi wa Nihon-go to Tai-go ga hanasemasu.
2. Yūbe yoku neraremasendeshita.
3. Watashi no heya kara umi ga miemasu.
4. Jidōsha no oto ga kikoemasu.

Kaiwa

Cortez:	1-ji made ni Shin-Ōsaka e ikemasu ka.
Tanaka:	Daijōbu desu.
	Koko kara 20-pun de ikemasu.
Cortez:	Kippu wa sugu kaemasu ka.
Tanaka:	Itsu demo kaemasu.
Cortez:	Shinkansen no naka de shokuji ga dekimasu ka.
Tanaka:	Ē, shokudō ga arimasu kara, dekimasu.
Cortez:	Sō desu ka.
Tanaka:	Denwa mo arimasu yo.
	Tōkyō ya Ōsaka ni kakeraremasu.
Cortez:	Sore wa benri desu ne.

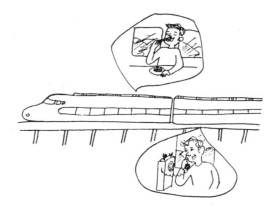

Reibun

1. Anata wa kanji ga yomemasu ka.
   —Hai, sukoshi yomemasu.
   —Iie, zenzen yomemasen.

2. Anata wa donokurai oyogemasu ka.
   —500-mētoru gurai oyogemasu.

3. Ashita 6-ji ni okiraremasu ka.
   —Hai, okirareru to omoimasu.
   —Iie, okirarenai to omoimasu.

4. Ashita mata koraremasu ka.
   —Hai, koraremasu.
   —Iie, koraremasen.

5. Anata wa terebi ga shūri-dekimasu ka.
   —Iie, dekimasen.

6. Anata wa Nihon-jin no namae ga oboeraremasu ka.
   —Iie, muzukashikute, oboeraremasen.

7. Kono mizu wa nomemasu.

8. Kono sakana wa taberaremasen.

9. Gohan ga dekimashita.

10. Atarashii michi ga dekimashita.

Renshū A

Dai I Gurūpu

1.

i**ki**	masu	i**ke**masu
ka**ki**	masu	
aru**ki**	masu	
oyo**gi**	masu	
yo**mi**	masu	
hai**ri**	masu	
suwa**ri**	masu	
ma**chi**	masu	
a**i**	masu	
ka**i**	masu	
hara**i**	masu	
nao**shi**	masu	
hana**shi**	masu	

Dai II Gurūpu

ne**masu**	ne**rare**masu
ake**masu**	
tabe**masu**	
tome**masu**	
oboe**masu**	
oshie**masu**	
oki**masu**	
kari**masu**	

Dai III Gurūpu

shimasu	**deki**masu
unten-**shi**masu	
kekkon-**shi**masu	
kimasu	**korare**masu
motte **ki**masu	

2. 1) Watashi wa Tai-go ga hanasemasu.
    kanji   yomemasu.
    piano   hikemasu.
    rajio   kumitateraremasu.
    terebi   shūri-dekimasu.

2) Umi   ga miemasu.
   Koe   kikoemasu.
   Gohan   dekimashita.

3) Kono mizu   wa nomemasu.
        sakana   taberaremasu.
        taipu   tsukaemasen.

Renshū B

1. Rei 1: kanji o yomimasu — kanji ga yomemasu
   Rei 2: yoku nemasen — yoku neraremasen
   1) o-sake o nomimasu —
   2) jidōsha o unten-shimasu —
   3) 1000-mētoru oyogimasu —
   4) sakana o tabemasu —
   5) Nihon no uta o utaimasu —
   6) Nihon-jin no namae o oboemasen —
   7) tabako o yamemasen —
   8) koko kara soto e demasen —

2. 1) Rei: Koko kara Fujisan ga miemasu.
   (Tōkyō-tawā, watashi no uchi, kōen, umi,
   tomodachi no uchi, takai yama)
   2) Rei: Watashi no koe ga kikoemasu ka.
   (Rao-san no koe, jidōsha no oto, hikōki no oto,
   sensei no koe, rajio no oto, kodomo no koe)

3. Rei: aruku koto ga dekimasu — arukemasu
   1) Nihon-go o hanasu koto ga dekimasu —
   2) omoi nimotsu o motsu koto ga dekimasu —
   3) okane o harau koto ga dekimasen —
   4) kikai o tomeru koto ga dekimasu —
   5) Itsuka Nihon e kuru koto ga dekimasu —
   6) doa o akeru koto ga dekimasen —

4. Rei: Sentā kara Fujisan ga miemasu ka. (iie, zenzen)
   —Iie, zenzen miemasen.
   1) Anata wa nan-mētoru oyogemasu ka. (100-mētoru kurai) —
   2) Hiragana ga oboeraremasu ka. (hai, daitai) —
   3) Anata wa nani-go ga dekimasu ka. (Nihon-go shika) —
   4) Mō shokuji ga dekimashita ka. (iie, mada) —
   5) Yūbe yoku neraremashita ka. (iie, amari) —

Mondai

I. 1. Anata wa nani-go ga hanasemasu ka.

2. Yūbe yoku neraremashita ka.

3. 1000-en attara anata no kuni de donna mono ga kaemasu ka.

4. Nihon-jin no namae ga sugu oboeraremasu ka.

5. Anata no heya kara nani ga miemasu ka.

6. Ima jidōsha no oto ga kikoemasu ka.

7. Anata wa o-sake ga nomemasu ka.

8. Anata wa rajio ga shūri-dekimasu ka.

9. Mō Nihon-go de denwa ga kakeraremasu ka.

10. Kasetto no koshō ga naosemasu ka.

II. Rei:

Ano hito wa
{ I. itsu
  II. itsuka
  ○III. itsumo }
tabako o sutte imasu.

1. Anata wa
{ I. mō
  II. mada
  III. tabun }
gohan o tabemashita ka.

2. Rao-san wa
{ I. amari
  II. sugu
  III. zutto }
kimasu.

3. Kore wa
{ I. zenzen
  II. zenbu
  III. zenbu de }
Nihon-sei desu.

4. Nihon-go ga
{ I. dandan
  II. takusan
  III. konoaida }
jōzu ni narimashita.

5. Bangohan no ato de,
{ I. massugu
  II. chōdo
  III. yoku }
sanpo-shimasu.

6. Kinō wa
{ I. sukoshi
  II. sonnani
  III. taihen }
samukunakatta desu.

Fukushū B

Rei: Kono kikai o (naosu—naoshite) kudasai.

1. Ano hito wa itsumo (warau—   ) imasu.

2. Koko de gitā o (hiku—   ) mo ii desu ka.

3. Sono heya ni (hairu—   ) nai de kudasai.

4. Hon o (kau—   ) ni (iku—   ) tai desu.

5. Gohan o (taberu—   ) kara, nani o (suru—   ) masu ka.

6. Koko de kutsu o (nugu—   ) nakereba narimasen.

7. Sentā de (benkyō-suru—   ) ato de, kōjō e ikimasu.

8. Asa hayaku (okiru—   ) koto ga dekimasen.

9. Mada shinkansen ni (noru—   ) koto ga arimasen.

10. Shawā o (abiru—   ), sorekara nemashita.

11. Watashi wa eiga o (miru—   ) koto ga suki desu.

12. Watashi no heya wa (hiroi—   ), akarui desu.

13. Konban ame ga (furu—   ) kamo shiremasen kara,
    kasa o (motte iku—   ) hō ga ii desu.

14. Ea-mēru de (okuru—   ) to, mik-ka de tsukimasu.

15. Anata wa (hima—   ) toki, nani o shimasu ka.

16. Heya no naka ga (kurai—   ) narimashita.

17. Anata wa (kuru—   ) nakute mo ii desu.

18. (Wakaranai—   ) ra, sensei ni kiite kudasai.

19. O-sake o (yameru—   ) koto wa muzukashii desu.

20. (Dekakeru—   ) mae ni, denwa o (kakeru—   ) hō ga ii desu.

Dai 27 Ka

Bunkei

1. Watashi wa Kimura-san ni shashin o misete agemashita.
2. Tanom-san wa watashi ni shashin o misete kudasaimashita.
3. Watashi wa Tanom-san ni shashin o misete moraimashita.
4. Jūsho o oshiete kudasaimasen ka.
5. Sensei wa o-kaeri ni narimashita.
6. Dōzo o-hairi kudasai.
7. Tanaka-san wa ashita koko e 9-ji ni irasshaimasu.
8. Kimura-san wa sō osshaimashita.

Kaiwa

Tanaka : Yā, Tanom-san, shibaraku desu ne.
　　　　　Dōzo o-kake kudasai.
　　　　　Itsu kochira e irasshaimashita ka.
Tanom : Yūbe desu.
Tanaka : Sō desu ka. O-tsukare ni natta deshō.
　　　　　Yūbe wa yoku o-yasumi ni naremashita ka.
Tanom : Hai, kesa 10-ji made nemashita.
　　　　　Ima kara Tōkyō e ikimasu.
Tanaka : Mō 12-ji desu yo.
　　　　　Koko de hirugohan o meshiagarimasen ka.
Tanom : Hai, arigatō gozaimasu.

Reibun

1. Watashi no kamera o kashite agemashō ka.
   —Hai, kashite kudasai.

2. Dare ni tetsudatte moraimashita ka.
   —Lee-san ni tetsudatte moraimashita.

3. Kāten o shimete kudasaimasen ka.

4. Dōzo o-kake kudasai.

5. Cortez-san, uketsuke made oide kudasai.

6. Donokurai o-machi ni narimashita ka.
   —20-pun gurai machimashita.

7. Ashita koko e irasshaimasu ka.
   —Hai, kimasu.

8. Sengetsu Indoneshia e irasshaimashita ka.
   —Hai, ikimashita.

9. Ashita anata wa Sentā ni irasshaimasu ka.
   —Iie, imasen.

10. Sensei wa nan to osshaimashita ka.
    —[Sensei wa] "Minasan ni yoroshiku." to osshaimashita.

Renshū A

1. Watashi wa Lee-san ni   shashin o mise te   agemashita.
   (Rao)   kamera o kashi te
                          zasshi o okut te

2. Rao-san wa watashi ni   shashin o mise te   kudasaimashita.
           (Lee)   kamera o kashi te
                          zasshi o okut te

3. Watashi wa Rao-san ni   shashin o mise te   moraimashita.
   (Lee)   kamera o kashi te
                          zasshi o okut te

4. **Jūsho o oshie** te   kudasaimasen ka.
   Kagi o tot te
   Mado o ake te

5. Sensei wa   o-kaeri   ni narimashita.
                   o-machi
                   o-yomi

6. Dōzo   o-hairi   kudasai.
             o-kake
             o-machi

Renshū B

1 Ali-san: <u>Kamera o kashite agemashō</u> ka.
   Tanom-san: Hai, <u>kashite kudasai</u>.
   1) (setsumei-suru)
   2) (shashin o miseru)
   3) (jisho o katte kuru)
   4) (jūsho o oshieru)
   5) (takushii o yobu)

2. Ali-san: (Watashi wa) Tanom-san ni <u>kamera o kashite agemashita</u>.
   1) (setsumei-suru)
   2) (shashin o miseru)
   3) (jisho o katte kuru)
   4) (jūsho o oshieru)
   5) (takushii o yobu)

3. Tanom-san: Ali-san wa (watashi ni) <u>kamera o kashite kudasaimashita</u>.
   1) (setsumei-suru)
   2) (shashin o miseru)
   3) (jisho o katte kuru)
   4) (jūsho o oshieru)
   5) (takushii o yobu)

4. Tanom-san: (Watashi wa) Ali-san ni <u>kamera o kashite moraimashita</u>.
   1) (setsumei-suru)
   2) (shashin o miseru)
   3) (jisho o katte kuru)
   4) (jūsho o oshieru)
   5) (takushii o yobu)

5. Rei: Dare ni <u>tetsudatte</u> moraimashita ka. (Lee-san)
   —<u>Lee-san</u> ni tetsudatte moraimashita.

   1) (Nihon-go o oshieru   :   Rao-san)
   2) (taipu o kasu   :   Arora-san)
   3) (bangō o shiraberu   :   sensei)
   4) (mado o akeru   :   Slamet-san)
   5) (jidōsha o shūri-suru   :   kōjō no hito)

6. Rei: dōzo o-hairi kudasai — Dōzo haitte kudasai.

   1) dōzo o-nori kudasai —
   2) dōzo o-suwari kudasai —
   3) dōzo o-hanashi kudasai —
   4) sukoshi o-machi kudasai —
   5) koko de o-yasumi kudasai —

7. Rei: Kono shinbun o o-yomi ni narimashita ka.
        —Hai, yomimashita.

   1) O-tsukare ni narimashita ka. —
   2) Tanaka-san ni o-ai ni narimashita ka. —
   3) O-machi ni narimashita ka. —
   4) Kōhii o o-nomi ni narimasu ka. —
   5) Kyōto ni o-tomari ni narimashita ka. —

8. Rei: Itsu Nihon e irasshaimashita ka. (senshū)
        —Senshū kimashita.

   1) Donokurai Nihon ni irasshaimasu ka. (6-kagetsu) —
   2) Nani o meshiagarimasu ka. (kōcha) —
   3) Ashita doko e irasshaimasu ka. (Nara) —
   4) Okusan no o-namae wa nan to osshaimasu ka. (Kazuko) —
   5) Hiroshima e irasshatta koto ga arimasu ka. (hai) —

Mondai

I. 1. Anata wa dochira kara irasshaimashita ka.
   2. Ashita dochira e irasshaimasu ka.
   3. Donata ni ichiban o-ai ni naritai desu ka.
   4. Maiasa nani o meshiagarimasu ka.
   5. Donata ga Nihon-go o oshiete kudasaimashita ka.
   6. Okāsan no tanjōbi ni nani o katte agemasu ka.
   7. Kodomo no toki, tanjōbi ni nani o katte moraimashita ka.
   8. Dare ni anata no tokei o katte moraimashita ka.
   9. Ima dochira ni sunde irasshaimasu ka.
   10. Maiban yoku o-yasumi ni naremasu ka.

II. Rei:

Ame ga futte imasu. { I. Soshite / ○ II. Shikashi / III. Desukara } ikanakereba narimasen.

   1. 5-shūkan Nihon-go o benkyō-shimashita.
      { I. Sorekara / II. Keredomo / III. Desukara } ima sukoshi wakarimasu.

   2. Ali-san wa Kyōto e ikimashita.
      { I. Dakara / II. Soshite / III. Shikashi } shashin o takusan torimashita.

   3. Hajime ni Nihon-go o benkyō-shimashita.
      { I. Sorekara / II. Desukara / III. Soredewa } jisshū ni ikimashita.

   4. Nihon no eiga o mitai desu.
      { I. Soredemo / II. Keredomo / III. Nan demo } jikan ga arimasen.

   5. Kōjō no Nihon-go wa muzukashii desu.
      { I. Soshite / II. Korekara / III. Dakara } ii jisho ga hoshii desu.

Dai 28 Ka

—Joshi—

1. [wa]

    1) Watashi wa Lee desu.   (Dai 1 Ka)

2. [no]

  A: 1) Kore wa watashi no hon desu.   (2)
       2) Watashi wa Tōkyō-kikai no kenshūsei desu.   (3)
       3) Kore wa Nihon no tokei desu.   (3)
       4) Kore wa terebi no hon desu.   (3)

  B: 1) Kore wa watashi no desu.   (2)
       2) Chiisai no o kudasai.   (14)

3. [o]

    1) Gohan o tabemasu.   (6)
    2) Kaisha o yasumimasu.   (9)
    3) Heya o demasu.   (13)
    4) Densha o orimasu.   (16)
    5) Hashi o watarimasu.   (22)

4. [ga]

  A: 1) Watashi wa kodomo ga arimasu.   (9)
       2) Watashi wa banana ga suki desu.   (9)
       3) Watashi wa sakana ga kirai desu.   (9)
       4) Lee-san wa pinpon ga jōzu desu.   (9)
       5) Watashi wa dansu ga heta desu.   (9)
       6) Watashi wa Nihon-go ga wakarımasu.   (9)

7) Watashi wa kamera ga hoshii desu. (13)

8) Watashi wa okane ga irimasu. (16)

9) Watashi wa Nihon-go ga dekimasu. (18)

10) Watashi wa eiga ga mitai desu. (13)

11) Arora-san wa atama ga ii desu. (16)

B: 1) Kyōshitsu ni kenshūsei ga imasu. (10)

2) Kyōshitsu ni tsukue ga arimasu. (10)

C: 1) Rao-san ga ichiban wakai desu. (12)

2) Ame ga futte imasu. (14)

D: 1) Watashi no heya wa chiisai desu ga, kirei desu. (8)

2) Iroiro arimasu ga, donna tēpu-rekōdā ga ii desu ka. (14)

E: 1) Tomodachi ga kekkon-suru toki, nan to iimasu ka. (22)

2) Kore wa watashi ga totta shashin desu. (23)

5. [ni]

1) Maiasa 6-ji ni okimasu. (4)

2) Tomodachi ni tegami o kakimasu. (7)

3) Tanaka-san ni Nihon-go o naraimashita. (7)

4) Tomodachi ni aimasu. (8)

5) Koko ni hon ga arimasu. (10)

6) 1-shūkan ni 1-kai sentaku-shimasu. (11)

7) Shokudō e gohan o tabe ni ikimasu. (13)

8) Ano resutoran ni hairimashō. (13)

9) Lee-san wa sensei ni narimasu. (15)

10) Densha ni norimasu. (16)

6. [e]

1) Yokohama e (ni) ikimasu. (5)

7. [de]

    1) Hikōki de kimashita.   (5)

    2) Niwa de shashin o torimasu.   (6)

    3) Pen de tegami o kakimasu.   (7)

    4) Nihon-go de repōto o kakimasu.   (7)

8. [to]

  A: 1) Matchi to haizara wa doko desu ka.   (3)

  B: 1) Tomodachi to issho ni ikimasu.   (5)

9. [ya—nado]

    1) Koko ni hon ya nōto ya enpitsu nado ga arimasu.   (10)

10. [kara—made]

    1) 12-ji kara 1-ji made yasumimasu.   (4)

    2) Tōkyō kara Ōsaka made shinkansen de ikimasu.   (5)

11 [kara]

    1) Watashi wa onaka ga itai desu kara, heya de nemasu.   (9)

12. [ka]

  A: 1) Anata wa Tanom-san desu ka.   (1)

  B: 1) Ueno ka Asakusa ga ii desu.   (19)

13. [yori]

    1) Tōkyō wa Ōsaka yori ōkii desu.   (12)

14 [mo]

    A: 1) Ano hito wa kenshūsei desu. Soshite watashi mo   (1)
          kenshūsei desu.

    B: 1) Doko [e] mo ikimasen.   (5)
        2) Nani mo tabemasen.   (6)
        3) Dare mo imasen.   (10)

15. [demo]

        1) Nan demo ii desu.   (13)

16. [ne]

        1) Lee-san to onaji desu ne.   (3)

17. [yo]

        1) Suzuki-san desu yo.   (15)

Dai 29 Ka

—Dōshi etc. + Kōzoku-ku—

1	[masu]-kei + tai desu	nomitai desu	(Dai 13 Ka)
2.	[masu]-kei + ni ikimasu	nomi ni ikimasu	(13)
3.	o + [masu]-kei + ni narimasu	o-nomi ni narimasu	(27)
4.	o + [masu]-kei + kudasai	o-nomi kudasai	(27)
5.	te-kei + kudasai	kaite kudasai	(14)
6.	te-kei + imasu	kaite imasu	(14)
7	te-kei + mo ii desu	kaite mo ii desu	(15)
8.	te-kei + kara,—	kaite kara, nemasu	(16)
9	te-kei + mo,—	kaite mo, wakarimasen	(25)
10.	te-kei + agemasu	kaite agemasu	(27)
11.	te-kei + kudasaimasu	kaite kudasaimasu	(27)
12.	te-kei + moraimasu	kaite moraimasu	(27)
13.	[nai]-kei + nai de kudasai	ikanai de kudasai	(17)
14.	[nai]-kei + nakereba narimasen (nai to ikemasen)	ikanakereba narimasen (ikanai to ikemasen)	(17)
15.	[nai]-kei + nakute mo ii desu	ikanakute mo ii desu	(17)
16.	jisho-kei + koto ga dekimasu	taberu koto ga dekimasu	(18)
17	jisho-kei + mae ni,—	taberu mae ni, araimasu	(18)
18.	jisho-kei } nai-kei } + to,—	taberu to, genki ni narimasu tabenai to, byōki ni narimasu	(22) (22)
19.	jisho-kei + koto ga suki desu	taberu koto ga suki desu	(24)

20. **ta-kei** + koto ga arimasu · · · · · · · yonda koto ga arimasu · · · · · · (19)

21. **ta-kei** ⎫
    ⎬ **+ hō ga ii desu** · · · · · · · yonda hō ga ii desu · · · · · · (19)
    nai-kei ⎭ · · · · · · · yomanai hō ga ii desu · · · · · · (19)

22. **ta-kei** + ato de,— · · · · · · · yonda ato de, nemasu · · · · · · (19)

23. **futsū-kei** + to omoimasu · (21)

24. **dōshi** ⎫
    ⎬ **futsū-kei**
    i-keiyōshi ⎭
                    · · · · · · · · · ·   deshō · · · · · · (21)
                    dewa nai   +
    meishi, na-keiyōshi ⎨   kamo shiremasen · · · · (21)
                    datta
                    dewa nakatta

25. **dōshi** ⎫
    ⎬ **futsū-kei**
    i-keiyōshi ⎭
               no
               dewa nai   toki,— · · · · · · (22)
    meishi ⎨ datta   + hito, etc. · · · · · · (23)
               dewa nakatta   **(meishi)**
                    na   koto · · · · · · · · · (24)
                    dewa nai
    na-keiyōshi ⎨ datta
                    dewa nakatta

26. **futsū-kei · kako** + ra,— · (25)

Dai 30 Ka

—Dōshi, Keiyōshi no Iroirona Tsukai-kata—

1. hayai desu (**i-keiyōshi**) . . . . hayaku (**fukushi**)

   Reı: hayai desu . . . . hayaku arukimasu

   osoi desu . . . . osoku kaerimasu

   ii desu . . . . yoku wakarimasu

   isogashii desu . . . . isogashiku hatarakimasu

2. shizuka desu (**na-keiyōshi**) . . . . shizuka ni (**fukushi**)

   Rei: shızuka desu . . . . shizuka ni hanashimasu

   kirei desu . . . . kirei ni sōji-shimasu

   shinsetsu desu . . . . shinsetsu ni oshiemasu

   genki desu . . . . genki ni asobimasu

3. yasumimasu (**dōshi**) . . . . yasumi (**meishi**)

   Rei: yasumimasu . . . . Kyō wa yasumi desu.

   ikimasu . . . . Ano densha wa Tōkyō-iki desu.

   hanashimasu . . . . Sensei no hanashi o kikimashita.

   hajimemasu . . . . Hajime kara yonde kudasai.

   owarimasu . . . . Kongetsu no owari ni kaerimasu.

4. omoi desu (**i-keiyōshi**) . . . . omosa (**meishi**)

   Rei: omoi desu . . . . Kono kaban no omosa wa 5 kg desu.

   takai desu . . . . Tōkyō-tawā no takasa wa 333 m desu.

   nagai desu . . . . Enpitsu no nagasa wa donokurai
   desu ka.

   hayai desu . . . . Shinkansen no hayasa wa 1-jikan ni
   163 km desu.

5. yomimasu (**dōshi**) .... yomi-kata (**meishi**)

Rei: yomimasu .... Kanji no <u>yomi-kata</u> ga wakarimasen.

tsukurimasu .... Indo-ryōri no <u>tsukuri-kata</u> o shitte imasu ka.

kakimasu................. Tegami no <u>kaki-kata</u> o oshiete kudasai.

tsukaimasu .... Taipu no <u>tsukai-kata</u> ga wakarimasu ka.

6. ōkii desu (**i-keiyōshi**)................. ōkiku⎫

shizuka desu (**na-keiyōshi**) .... shizuka <u>ni</u>⎬ narimasu

12-ji desu (**meishi**) .... 12-ji <u>ni</u>⎭

Rei: Kodomo wa dandan <u>ōkiku narimashita</u>.

Pātii ga owattara, <u>shizuka ni narimashita</u>.

Watashi wa sengetsu <u>20-sai ni narimashita</u>.

7. hayai desu (**i-keiyōshi**) .... hayaku⎫

shizuka desu (**na-keiyōshi**) .... shizuka <u>ni</u>⎬ shimasu

ashita desu (**meishi**) .... ashita <u>ni</u>⎭

Rei: Jikan ga arimasen kara, <u>hayaku shite</u> kudasai.

Ima benkyō-shite imasu kara, <u>shizuka ni shite</u> kudasai.

Kyō wa isogashii desu kara, <u>ashita ni shimashō</u>.

Sakura, sakura

(Cherry blossoms)

Andante ♩ = 63

Sa - ku - ra,   sa - ku - ra,   Ya - yo - i   no
Sa - ku - ra,   sa - ku - ra!   'Gainst the   A - pril

so - ra___ wa   Mi - wa - ta - su   ka - gi - ri   Ka - su - mi ka
skies a - far,   Cher - ry blos - soms   scat - ter'd___ are,   Mist or cloud you

dimi------ nu ----- endo

ku - mo___ ka   Ni - o - i   zo   i - zu - ru   I - za - ya
might as - sume   'Til you smell their sweet per - fume.   Come with me,

morendo

i - za - ya   Mi ni   yu - ka - n.
come with me,   The fair cher - ry flow'rs   to see!

Kōjō no tsuki

(Moon on the ruined castle)

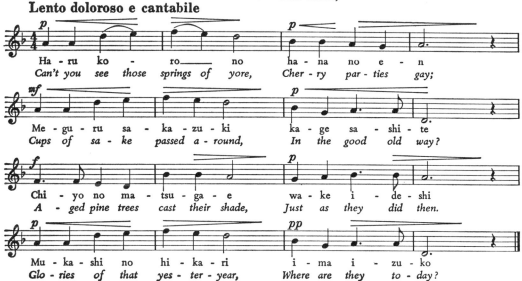

Lento doloroso e cantabile

Ha - ru ko - ro_____ no ha - na no e - n
Can't you see those springs of yore, Cher - ry par - ties gay;

Me - gu - ru sa - ka - zu - ki ka - ge sa - shi - te
Cups of sa - ke passed a - round, In the good old way?

Chi - yo no ma - tsu - ga - e wa - ke i - de - shi
A - ged pine trees cast their shade, Just as they did then.

Mu - ka - shi no hi - ka - ri i - ma i - zu - ko
Glo - ries of that yes - ter - year, Where are they to - day?

2. **Aki jinei no shimo no iro**
   Naki yuku kari no kazu misete
   Uuru tsurugi ni terisoishi
   Mukashi no hikari ima izuko

3. Ima kōjō no yowa no tsuki
   Kawaranu hikari **ta** ga tamezo
   Kaki ni nokoru **wa** tada kazura
   Matsu **ni** utau **wa** tada arashi

4. Tenjō kage wa kawaranedo
   Eiko wa utsuru yo no sugata
   Utsusan tote **ka** ima mo nao
   Ā kōjō no yowa no tsuki

Hamabe no uta

(The song of the beach)

2. Yūbe hamabe o motooreba
    Mukashi no hito zo shinobaruru
    Yosuru nami yo, kaesu nami yo
    Tsuki no iro mo, hoshi no kage mo

    O when I wander on the shore
    At night, when day is done,
    Fond memories come back to me
    Of people who are gone.
    O listen to the breakers,
    The waves that come and go
    Beneath the moon's pale yellow light
    And by the starlight's glow.

Akatonbo

(The scarlet dragon-fly)

2. Yama no hatake no kuwanomi o
   Kokago ni tsunda wa maboroshi ka

   Was it true, or did I dream it?
   High upon the hill,
   We were picking mulberries, and I
   Just a baby still.

3. Jūgo de nēya wa yome ni yuki
   Osato no tayori mo taehateta

   Nanny went away to marry:
   She was scarce fifteen.
   What has happened to the village now,
   In the years between?

4. Yūyake koyake no akatonbo
   Tomatte iru yo sao no saki

   Still I see that scarlet dragon-fly
   In the setting sun,
   On a slender tip of young bamboo,
   Just as day was done.

Sakuin

—G—

ga 8
gaikoku 11
gakkō 10
Ganbatte kudasai 24
genki (-na) 8
[*O-*]*genki desu ka* 5
[*Dōzo*] *o-genki de* 18
getsu-yōbi 4
ginkō 5
gitā 9
-go 3
Gochisōsama 21
go-gatsu 5
gogo 4
gohan 6
Gomen kudasai 17
goro 12
gozen 4
gurai (kurai) *11*
gyūniku 9
gyūnyū (miruku) 6

—H—

ha 16
hachi-gatsu 5
hai 1
Hai, dōzo 2
hairimasu [heya ni —] (hairu) 13
haizara 2
hajimemasu (hajimeru) 6
Hajimemashite, dōzo yoroshiku 19
hajime ni 25
hakkiri 14
hako 2
han 4
hana 6
hana 16
hanashimasu (hanasu) 14

hansamu(-na) 8
haraimasu (harau) 16
hashi 7
hashi 22
hatarakimasu (hataraku) 4
hayai 12
hayaku 14
hayaku 17
heta(-na) 9
heya 3
hidari 10
hijōni 21
hikimasu [gitā o —] (hiku) 18
hikimasu (hiku) 25
hikōki 5
hikui 8
hima(-na) 12
hiragana 9
hiroi 16
hiru 4
hirugohan 6
hito 5
hitori 11
hitori de 5
hitotsu 11
hoka ni 23
hon 2
Hontō desu ka 24
hoshii 13
hon-ya 5
hoteru 19
hyaku 2
hyaku-man 3

—I—

ichiban 12
ichi-gatsu 5
ichi-man 3
ichinichi-jū 25
Igirisu 3

oshimasu (osu)   25
osoi   12
osoku   17
Ōsutoraria   1
otearai   3
oto   16
otoko no hito   10
otōsan   7
otōto   7
ototoi   4
owarimasu (owaru)   6
owari ni   25
Oyasuminasai   7
o-yasumi nı narimasu   27
oyogimasu (oyogu)   18

—P—

pan   6
pasupōto   10
pātii   21
pen   2
penchi   7
Perū   1
pinpon-shimasu (pinpon-suru)   6
posuto   10
-pun   4
purēyā   16

—R—

rajio   2
raigetsu   5
rainen   5
raishū   5
ranpu   25
rekōdo   6
repōto   7
resutoran   10
ringo   6
robii   3
roku-gatsu   5

rōmaji   9
ryōhō   12
ryokō   12
ryōri   9

—S—

sā   23
sabishii   22
-sai   2
sakana   6
[o-]sake   6
sakura   8
samui   8
-san   1
san-gatsu   5
san-nin   11
sanpo-shimasu (sanpo-suru)   13
satō   14
sawarimasu (sawaru)   17
Sayōnara   7
se ga takai   16
[Nihon-]sei   11
seihın   21
sekai   12
sekken   15
semai   16
sen   3
sengetsu   5
senmon   2
sensei   1
senshū   5
[Kenshū] Sentā   3
sentaku-shimasu (sentaku-suru)   11
sētā   22
setsumei-shimasu (setsumei-suru)   24
shashin   6
shatsu   6
shi-gatsu   5
Shibaraku desu ne   17
shichi-gatsu   5

日 本 語 の 基 礎 Ⅰ
＜本冊ローマ字版＞

1972年12月1日　初版発行
1990年9月10日　第 13 刷

編　集　　財団法人 海 外 技 術 者 研 修 協 会

発　行　　株式会社 スリーエー ネットワーク
　　　　　東京都千代田区猿楽町2丁目6番3号
　　　　　電話 (03) 292-5751(代表)松栄ビル
　　　　　郵便番号 101

印　刷　　奥 村 印 刷 株 式 会 社

日本音楽著作権協会（出）許諾第8211650号

Chāto 1

No.	namae	yomikata
1	Tanom	Tanomu
2	Abebe	Abebe
3	Cortez	Korutesu
4	Kimura	
5	Lee	Rii
6	Rao	Rao
7	Slamet	Surametto
8	Garcia	Garushia
9	Tanaka	
	Ali	Ari
	Katō	
	Arora	Arōra

Chāto 1

Chāto 2

1 kagi	2 pen	3 kami
4 haizara	5 nōto	6 hako
7 jisho	8 isu	9 tsukue

Chāto 2

1	2	3
hon	enpitsu	kaban
4	5	6
matchi	rajio	terebi
7	8	9
zasshi	tokei	shinbun
10	11	12
kamera	tabako	jidōsha

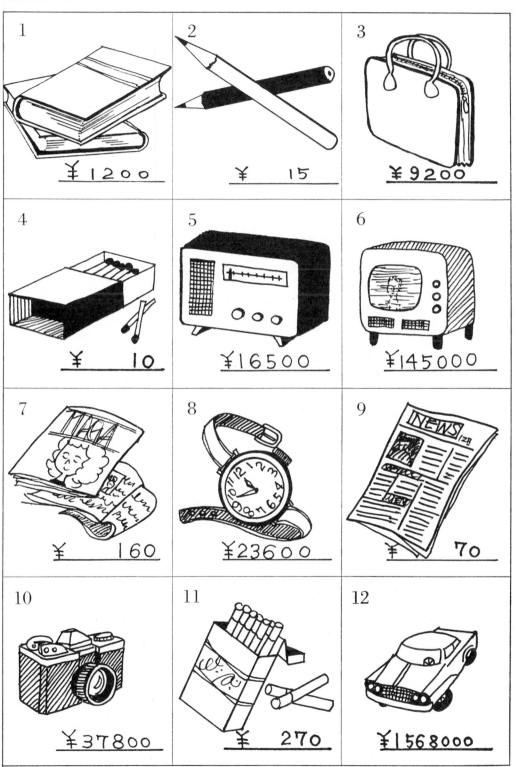

1 ku-ji	7 san-ji	1 yo-ji go-fun	6 yo-ji yonjippun
2 jū-ji	8 yo-ji	2 yo-ji jippun	7 yo-ji gojūgo-fun
3 jūichi-ji	9 go-ji	3 yo-ji jūgo-fun	8 chōdo go-ji
4 jūni-ji	10 roku-ji	4 yo-ji {sanjippun {han	9 gozen go-ji
5 ichi-ji	11 nana-ji (shichi-ji)	5 yo-ji sanjūgo-fun	10 gogo ku-ji
6 ni-ji	12 hachi-ji		

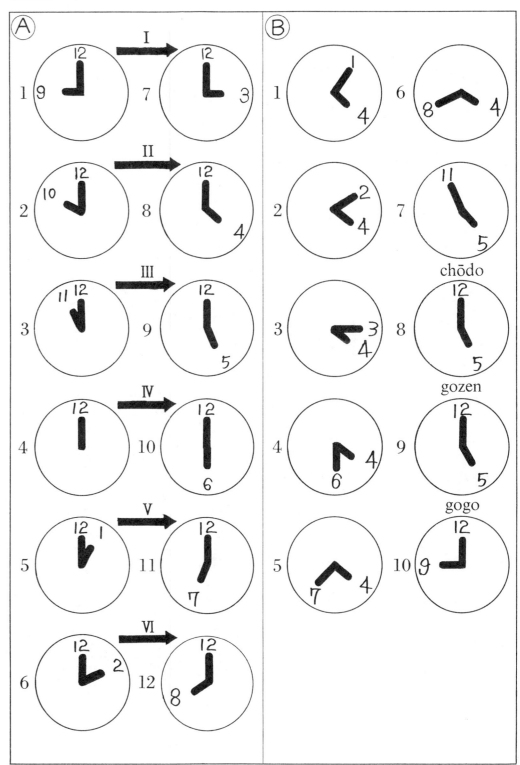

1 gohan o tabemasu	2 hana o kaimasu
3 tabako o suimasu	4 kōhii o nomimasu
5 shashin o torimasu	6 rekōdo o kikimasu
7 hon o yomimasu	8 tegami o kakimasu
9 terebi o mimasu	10 Nihon-go o benkyō-shimasu

1 denwa o kakemasu	2 takushii o yobimasu	3 10-ji ni nemasu
4 isogimasu	5 uchi e kaerimasu	6 heya de yasumimasu
7 shatsu o sentaku-shimasu	8 rajio o shūri-shimasu	9 Nihon-go de hanashimasu

Chāto 7

1 mado o akemasu	2 mado o shimemasu
3 terebi o tsukemasu	4 terebi o keshimasu
5 Ali-san ni hon o agemasu	6 Rao-san kara hon o moraimasu
7 haizara o okimasu	8 haizara o torimasu
9 kagi o iremasu	10 kagi o dashimasu

Chāto   8

1	2	3
asa 6-ji ni okimasu	gohan o tabemasu	kyōshitsu e kimasu
4	**5**	**6**
heya ni hairimasu	mado o akemasu	heya o sōji-shimasu
7	**8**	**9**
Tōkyō e ikimasu	tomodachi ni aimasu	issho ni sanpo-shimasu
10	**11**	**12**
Tōkyō de densha ni norimasu	Yokohama de densha o orimasu	kōjō made arukimasu

1 shinbun o 　yomimasu	tegami o 　kakimasu	6 kekkon- 　shimasu	Nihon e 　kimasu
2 sentaku-shimasu	pinpon-shimasu	7 naoshimasu	unten-shimasu
3 benkyō-shimasu	asobimasu	8 doa o 　nokku-shimasu	heya ni 　hairimasu
4 okane o 　haraimasu	eiga o mimasu	9 shawā o 　abimasu	nemasu
5 denki o 　keshimasu	heya o demasu	10 te o araimasu	gohan o 　tabemasu